MW01711777

# Difficult Puzzle Book For Smart Kids

## Over 240 Brain Games For 8 Year Olds

M. Prefontaine

Published by Horizon Books

# Contents

# Introduction

This puzzle book contains over 240 brainteasers of all sorts for you to try and solve, ranging from number logic puzzles to word riddles, to classic games and to some all new puzzles.

These puzzles are designed to be particularly challenging, so don't feel bad if you can't complete some of them: you will naturally be better at some types of puzzles than others. Try using a pencil so that you can make any corrections if you go wrong.

Each puzzle has a correct solution, but some puzzles may have more than one: use the answers as a guide, as your answer may also follow all the rules and be correct.

Try your best, and good luck, but most importantly, remember to have fun!

# 1. Linesweeper

The aim of this game is to draw a single loop throughout the puzzle made of just straight lines.

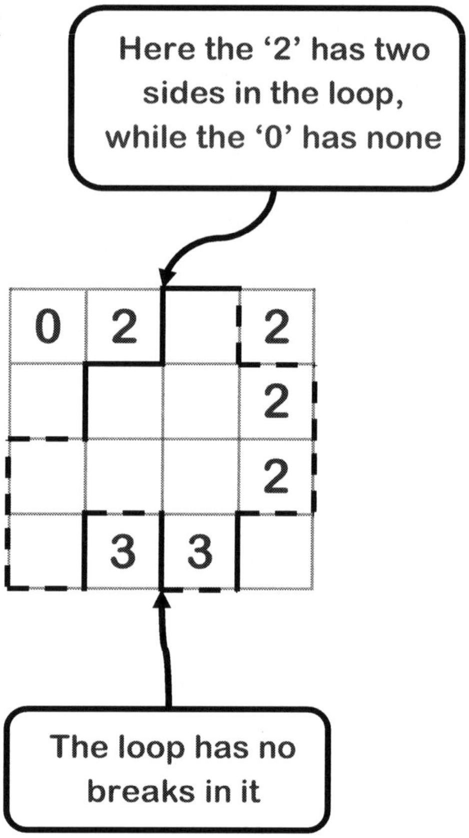


**The Rules**

- The loop has to use all the lines already in
- Each number shows how many sides of that box are included in the loop
- The loop cannot touch or cross over itself

Use this example as a guide to help you attempt the others.

A)

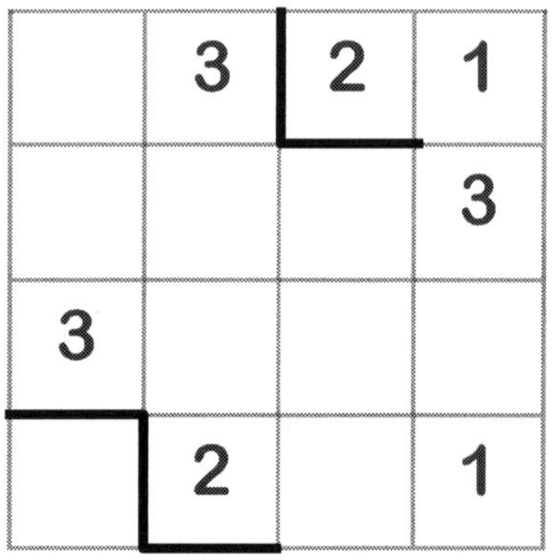


B)

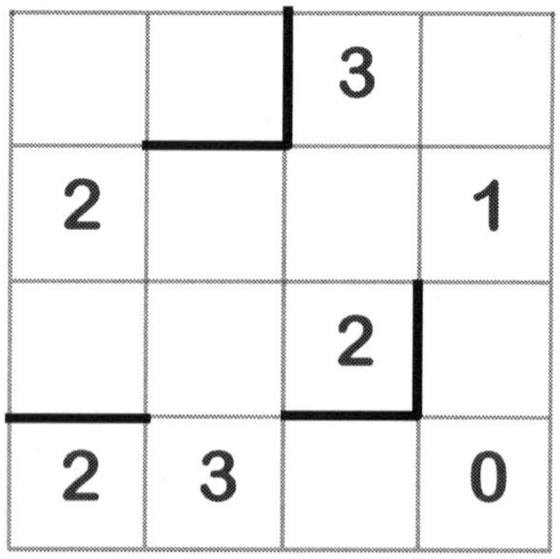

C)

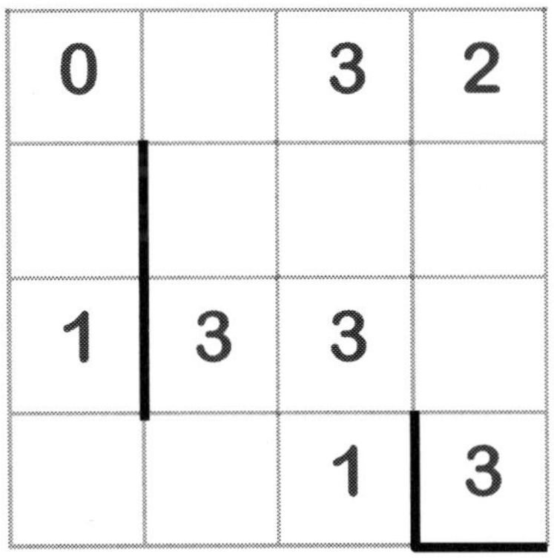


D)

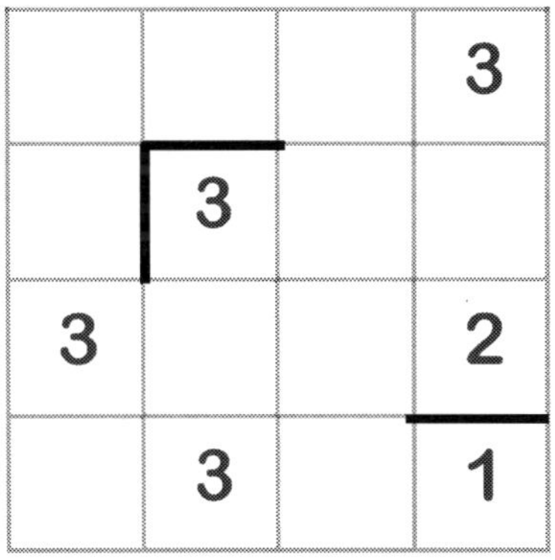


If you are struggling, try to solve each number individually, so that they all link together

E)

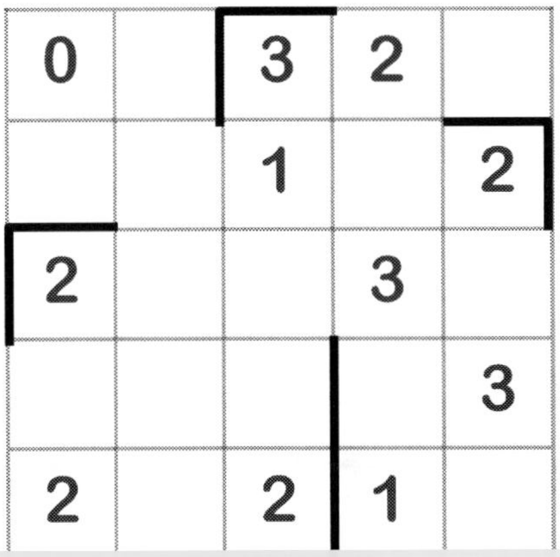


F)

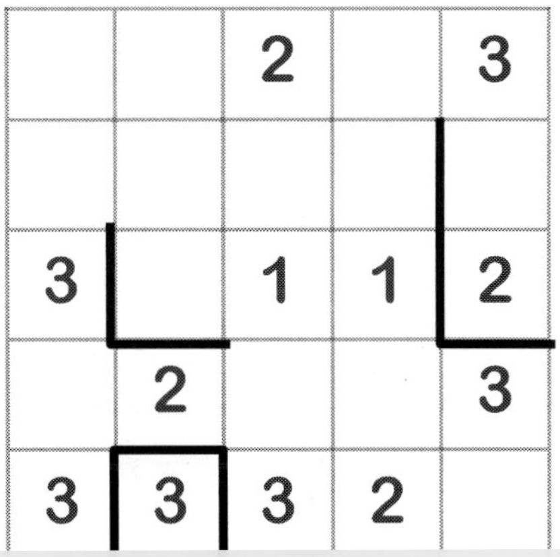

# 2. Word Ladder

**Can you change the top word to the bottom by changing one letter at a time?**

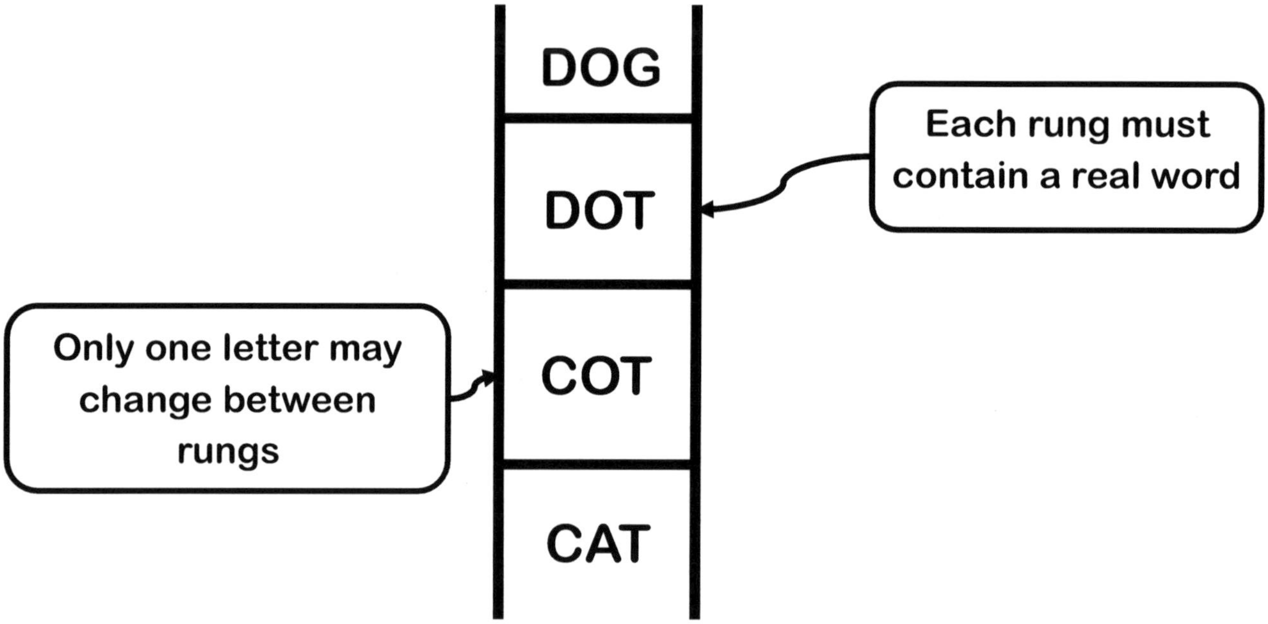


**A)**

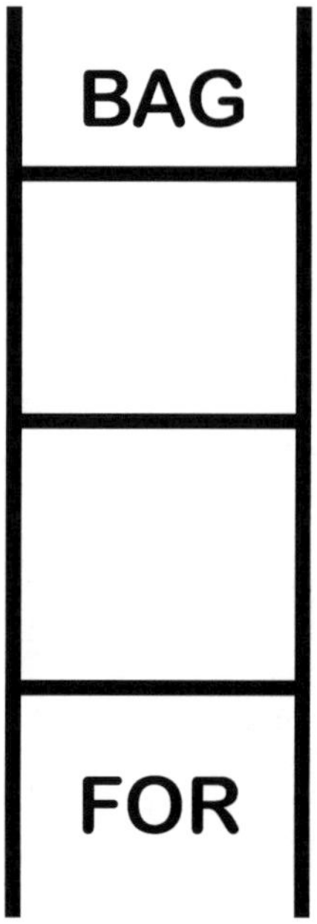


**B)**

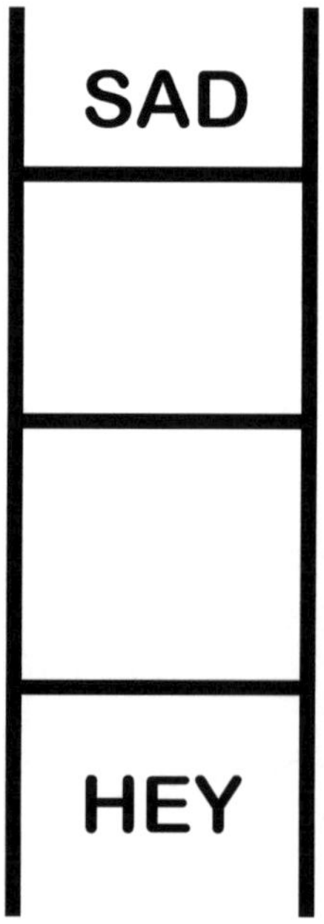

C)

LEG

MAP

D)

PAY

RED

E)

BUSH

CAKE

F)

MICE

LAMP

# 3. Sudoku

Sudoku is a Japanese puzzle where you have to fill out the remaining numbers using the numbers already in the grid.

## The Rules

- Every row, column, and small box must have 1-6, or 1-9 in
- No number can be repeated in any part
- The numbers already in are correct, which will help you fill in the rest

Each smaller box is marked by the bold lines

| | | | | | |
|---|---|---|---|---|---|
| 5 | 6 | 3 | 2 | 1 | 4 |
| 2 | 1 | 4 | 6 | 3 | 5 |
| 6 | 3 | 1 | 4 | 5 | 2 |
| 4 | 2 | 5 | 6 | 3 | 1 |
| 3 | 5 | 2 | 1 | 4 | 6 |
| 1 | 4 | 6 | 5 | 3 | 2 |

Use the completed example to help you try and solve the others.

A)

| | | | | | |
|---|---|---|---|---|---|
| | | 3 | | 1 | |
| 5 | 6 | | 3 | 2 | |
| | 5 | 4 | 2 | | 3 |
| 2 | | 6 | 4 | 5 | |
| | 1 | 2 | | 4 | 5 |
| | 4 | | 1 | | |

B)

| | | | | | |
|---|---|---|---|---|---|
| 6 | 4 | | 2 | | |
| | 5 | 1 | | | |
| 3 | 6 | 4 | | | 2 |
| 5 | | | 4 | 3 | 6 |
| | | | 6 | 4 | |
| | | 6 | | 2 | 5 |

C)

| | | | | | | | | |
|---|---|---|---|---|---|---|---|---|
| | | 7 | 6 | 5 | | | | |
| | 3 | 1 | | 7 | | | | |
| | | 6 | | | 8 | 4 | | 9 |
| 6 | | | 4 | | | 3 | 5 | |
| | | 9 | | 1 | | 8 | | |
| | 1 | 3 | | | 6 | | | 7 |
| 7 | | 2 | 3 | | | 1 | | |
| | | | | 8 | | 5 | 3 | |
| | | | | 4 | 1 | 7 | | |

D)

| | | | | | | | | |
|---|---|---|---|---|---|---|---|---|
| | 9 | | 1 | | | | | |
| | 6 | 7 | 8 | | | | 3 | 4 |
| 1 | | | | | | | 9 | 6 |
| | | 2 | | 8 | 9 | | 1 | |
| | | | 6 | 7 | 2 | | | |
| | 7 | | 5 | 4 | | 3 | | |
| 4 | 3 | | | | | | | 1 |
| 8 | 5 | | | | 7 | 4 | 6 | |
| | | | | | 6 | | 5 | |

E)

| | | | | | | | | |
|---|---|---|---|---|---|---|---|---|
| | | | | | | | 7 | 6 |
| | | | | 2 | | 5 | | 1 |
| 5 | 9 | 6 | 4 | | | | | |
| | 8 | | 6 | 1 | | | 3 | |
| 6 | | 7 | | | | 8 | | 5 |
| | 3 | | | 4 | 5 | | 2 | |
| | | | | | 8 | 1 | 4 | 2 |
| 8 | | 2 | | 5 | | | | |
| 9 | 6 | | | | | | | |

F)

| | | | | | | | | |
|---|---|---|---|---|---|---|---|---|
| 8 | | | | 7 | 4 | | 6 | |
| | | | 8 | | | 1 | 9 | |
| | 2 | 1 | 5 | | 9 | | | |
| 4 | | | | | | | 1 | |
| | | 3 | 9 | | 5 | 7 | | |
| | 1 | | | | | | | 3 |
| | | | 6 | | 8 | 3 | 5 | |
| | 6 | 8 | | | 1 | | | |
| | 9 | | 7 | 3 | | | | 6 |

# 4. Atomic Words

**By picking one letter from each ring and working inwards, can you find all the words hidden in these puzzles?**

**For a challenge, see how many words you can find in five minutes.**

Pick your first letter from this outer ring, and continue to pick from the next one

A)

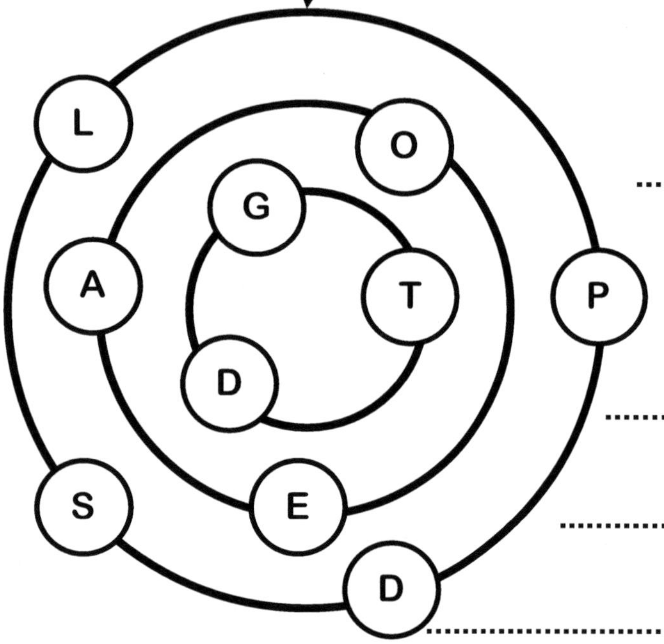

B)

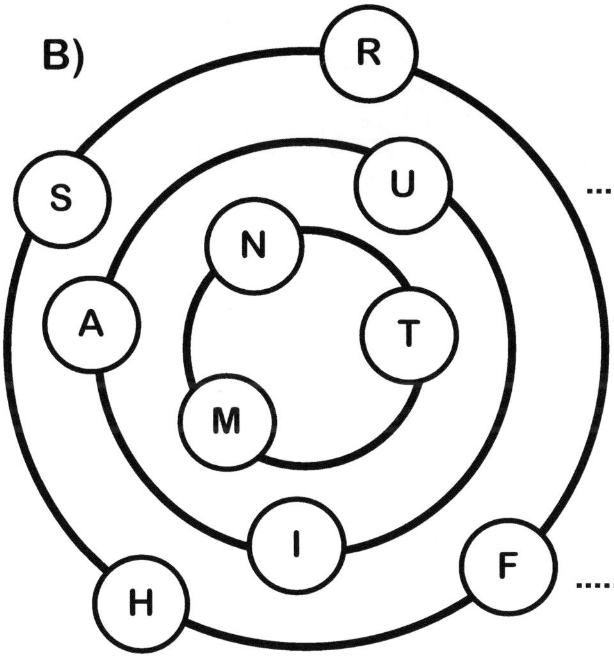


C)

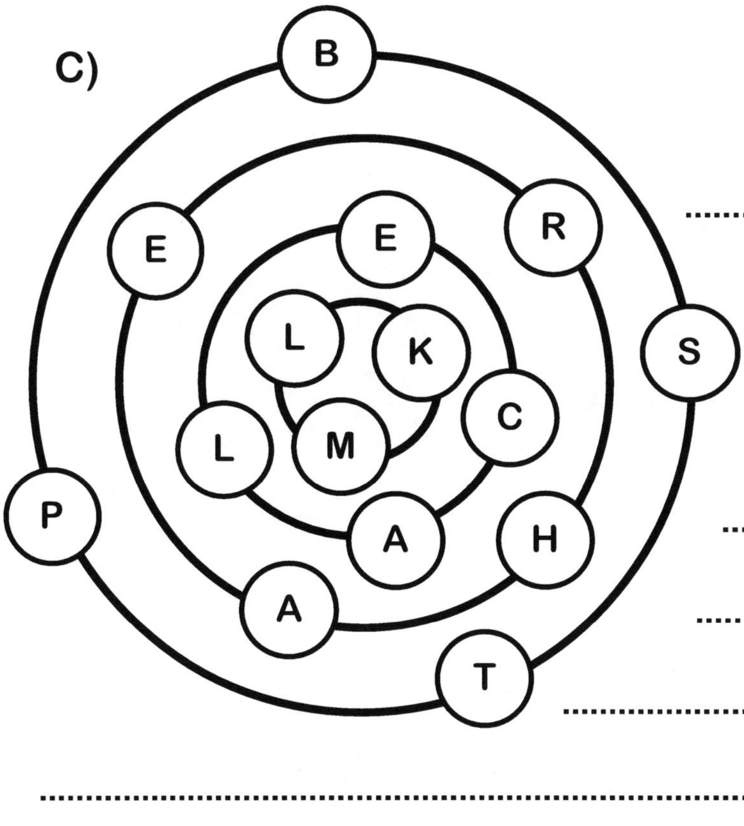

# 5. Balancing the Scales

Can you solve this logic puzzle, and find out which shapes are the heaviest, and lightest?

You may find it helpful to work out how much shapes weigh against other shapes.

A)

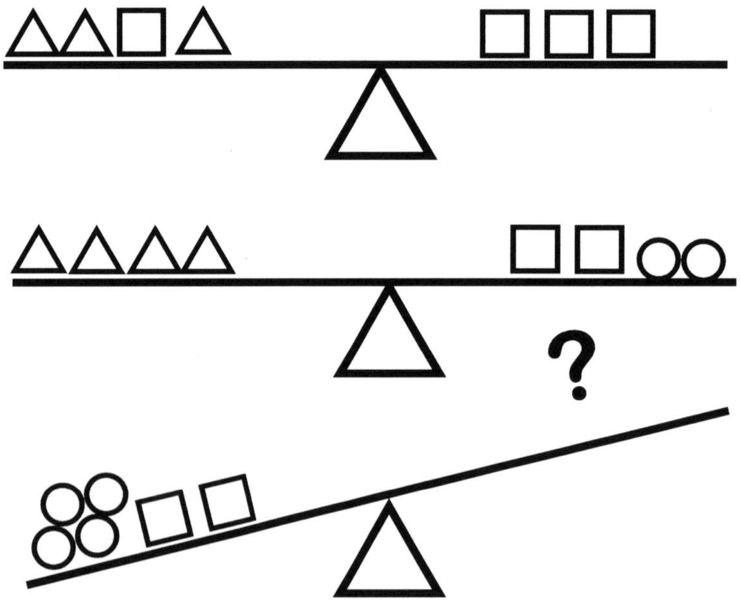


Which of these shapes are the heaviest?

Which shape is the lightest?

How many triangles are needed to balance the scales?

B)

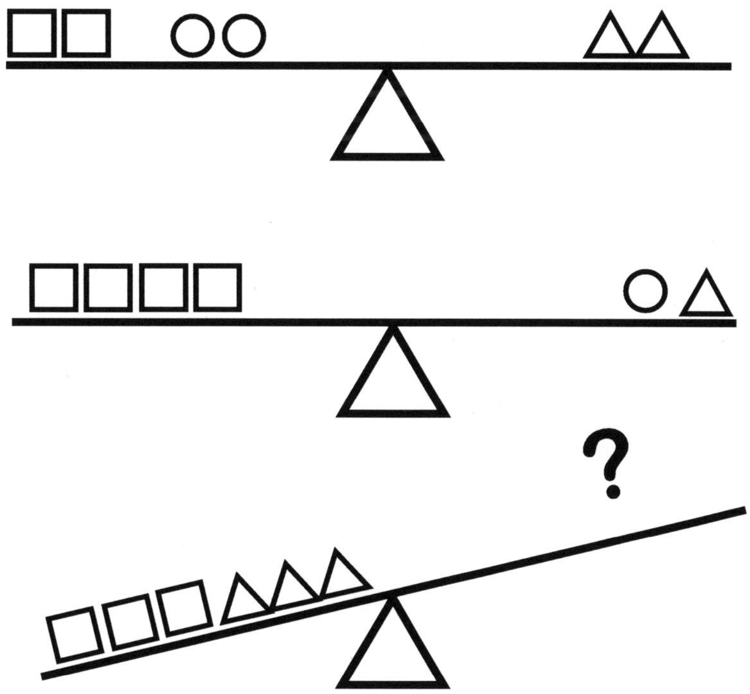

Which of these shapes are the heaviest?

Which shape is the lightest?

How many circles are needed to balance the scales?

What's the lowest numbers you could give to each

# 6. Letter Blocks

**Can you find the missing letters to complete the words in this tricky game?**

**<u>The Rules</u>**

- **Each puzzle has a 'letter block' to find, which when placed in, will complete all words**
- **E) has two letter blocks, each of which will complete three out of the six puzzles**

The 'ET' here completes both words: pet, and feet

| | |
|---|---|
| E | T |

| | | |
|---|---|---|
| P | E | T |

| | | | |
|---|---|---|---|
| F | E | E | T |

A)

| | |
|---|---|
| | |

| | | | |
|---|---|---|---|
| S | | | D |

| | | | | |
|---|---|---|---|---|
| C | L | | | M |

| | | | | | |
|---|---|---|---|---|---|
| P | R | | | S | E |

| | | | |
|---|---|---|---|
| G | | | N |

| | | | | |
|---|---|---|---|---|
| P | | | N | T |

| | | | | | |
|---|---|---|---|---|---|
| F | | | R | L | Y |

B)

| | |
|---|---|
| | |

| | | | |
|---|---|---|---|
| G | | | L |

| | | | | |
|---|---|---|---|---|
| B | | | R | D |

| | | | | | |
|---|---|---|---|---|---|
| T | H | R | | | T |

| | | | |
|---|---|---|---|
| T | | | D |

| | | | | |
|---|---|---|---|---|
| G | L | | | T |

| | | | | | |
|---|---|---|---|---|---|
| C | | | R | S | E |

C)

| | | |
|---|---|---|
| | | |

| | | | | |
|---|---|---|---|---|
| T | E | | | |

| | | | | | |
|---|---|---|---|---|---|
| M | | | | O | D |

| | | | | | | |
|---|---|---|---|---|---|---|
| W | H | | | | E | R |

| | | | | |
|---|---|---|---|---|
| | | | I | C |

| | | | | | |
|---|---|---|---|---|---|
| L | | | | A | L |

| | | | | | | |
|---|---|---|---|---|---|---|
| R | | | | I | N | K |

D)

| | | |
|---|---|---|
| | | |

| | | | | |
|---|---|---|---|---|
| | | | E | R |

| | | | | | |
|---|---|---|---|---|---|
| P | | | | E | S |

| | | | | | | |
|---|---|---|---|---|---|---|
| I | S | O | | | | E |

| | | | | |
|---|---|---|---|---|
| S | P | | | |

| | | | | | |
|---|---|---|---|---|---|
| F | | | | L | Y |

| | | | | | | |
|---|---|---|---|---|---|---|
| R | E | | | | E | D |

E)

| | |
|---|---|
| | |

| | |
|---|---|
| | |

| | | | |
|---|---|---|---|
| B | | | N |

| | | | | |
|---|---|---|---|---|
| | | I | N | G |

| | | | | | |
|---|---|---|---|---|---|
| R | H | Y | | | M |

| | | | |
|---|---|---|---|
| B | A | | |

| | | | | |
|---|---|---|---|---|
| S | H | | | T |

| | | | | | |
|---|---|---|---|---|---|
| B | E | F | | | E |

# 7. Magic Square

**Can you fill in these grids, and arrive at the magic number?**

**The Rules**

- Each row and column add up to the magic number, which is different in each puzzle
- Each number may only be used once from within the range given

Try your best with these puzzles.

1-9 are the numbers used in the answer

15 is the magic number

15

1-9

| | | |
|---|---|---|
| 4 | 8 | 3 |
| 9 | 1 | 5 |
| 2 | 6 | 7 |

A): 15
1-9

| | | |
|---|---|---|
| 9 | | 4 |
| | 7 | |
| | | |

B): 18
2-10

| | | |
|---|---|---|
| 2 | | 7 |
| | | |
| 6 | | |

C): 24
4-12

| | | | |
|---|---|---|---|
| | | 10 | ___ |
| 7 | 12 | | ___ |
| | | | ___ |
| ___ | ___ | ___ | |

D): 21
3-11

| | | | |
|---|---|---|---|
| 10 | | | ___ |
| | | | ___ |
| 6 | 11 | | ___ |
| ___ | ___ | ___ | |

E): 34
1-16

| | | | | |
|---|---|---|---|---|
| | 11 | | 1 | ___ |
| 13 | | 7 | | ___ |
| | | 9 | | ___ |
| | 5 | 4 | 15 | ___ |
| ___ | ___ | ___ | ___ | |

F): 38
2-17

| | | | | |
|---|---|---|---|---|
| 17 | | | 14 | ___ |
| | 11 | 12 | | ___ |
| 10 | 7 | | | ___ |
| | 16 | | 2 | ___ |
| ___ | ___ | ___ | ___ | |

# 8. Stolen Vowels

**Can you put the vowels back into these puzzles, and spell out each of the solutions?**

## A): European Countries

**NGLND**

**GRMNY**

**PRTGL**

**FRNC**

**SPN**

## B): Farm Animals

**SHP**

**GT**

**CHCKN**

**HRS**

**CW**

## C): Musical Instruments

TRMPT

SXPHN

CLRNT

VLN

HRP

## D): Sports

TNNS

BDMNTN

BSKTBLL

FTBLL

NTBLL

# 9. Kakuro

**Kakuro is a Japanese puzzle that focuses on addition. By using the clues within the grid, try and fill in the answers.**

## The Rules

- **Each clue number is the total sum of all numbers in that line**
- **If the clue is in the top segment, the line follows to the right. If it is in the bottom, it follows downwards**
- **You may use any number 1-9, but they cannot be repeated within the same line**

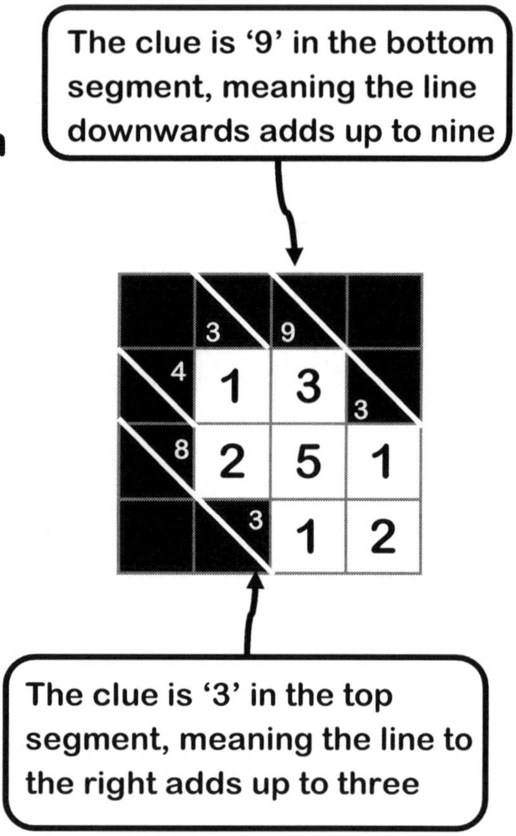


**Use the completed example as a guide to attempt the other puzzles.**

**A)**

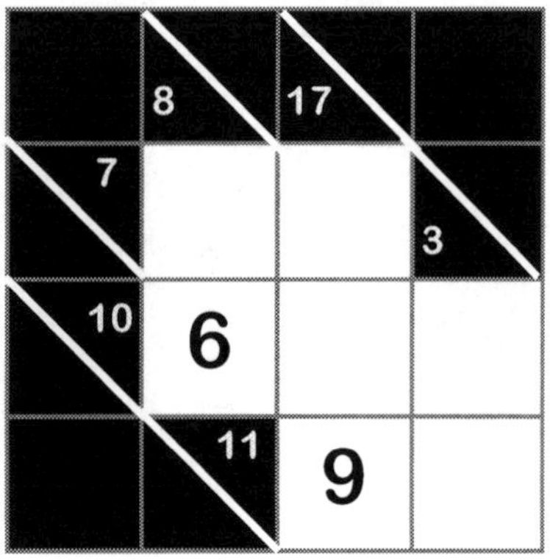


**B)**

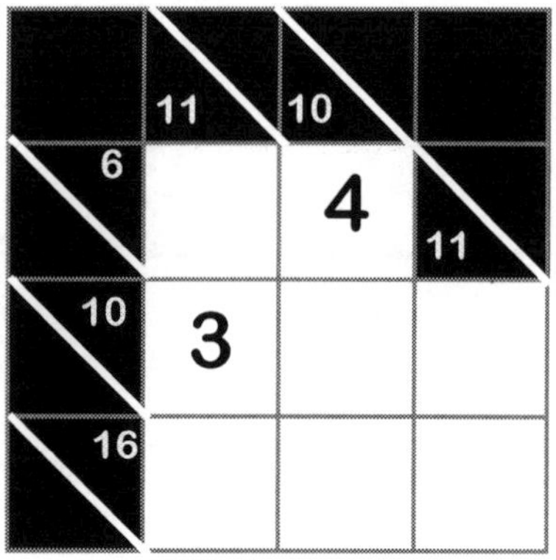

C)

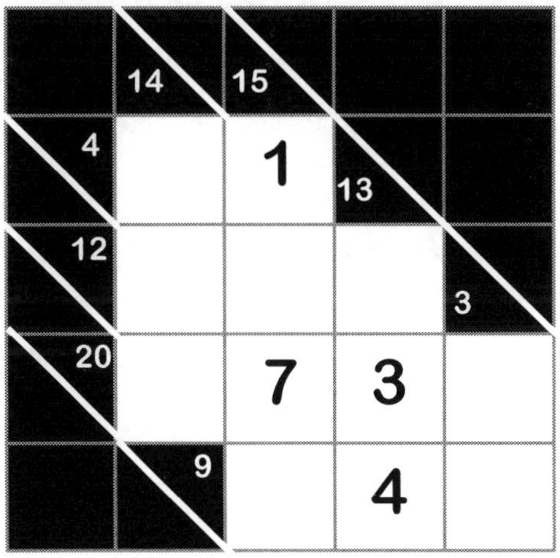


D)

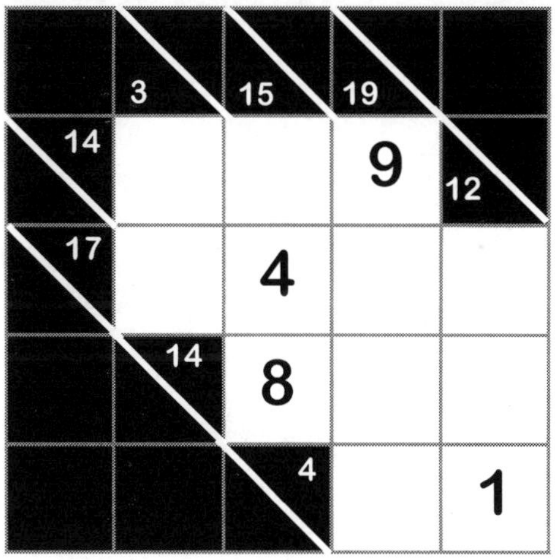


Try writing down possible combinations, and see where they could fit together with other clues

E)

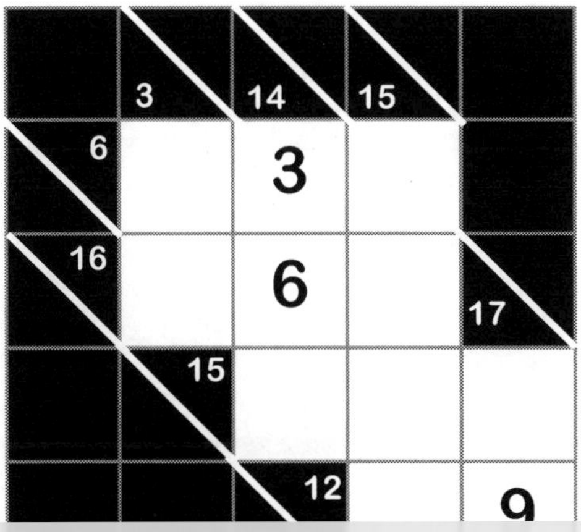


F)

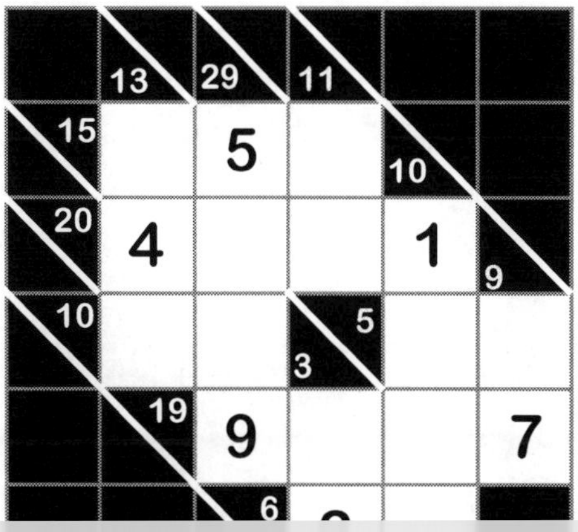

# 10. Making Connections

This game is all about connecting the same shapes together within the grid, using all the squares to solve the puzzle.

## The Rules

- Each pair of shapes must be connected together as shown
- The lines between shapes cannot touch or cross over each other
- Every square in the grid must be used

Use the example to help you attempt the other puzzles.

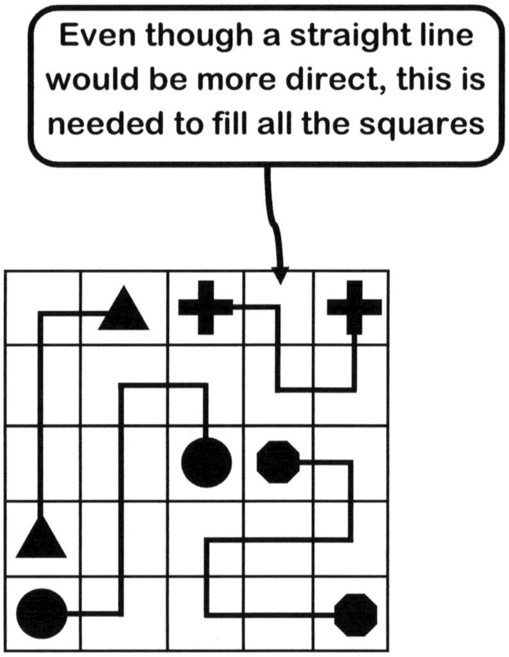


A)

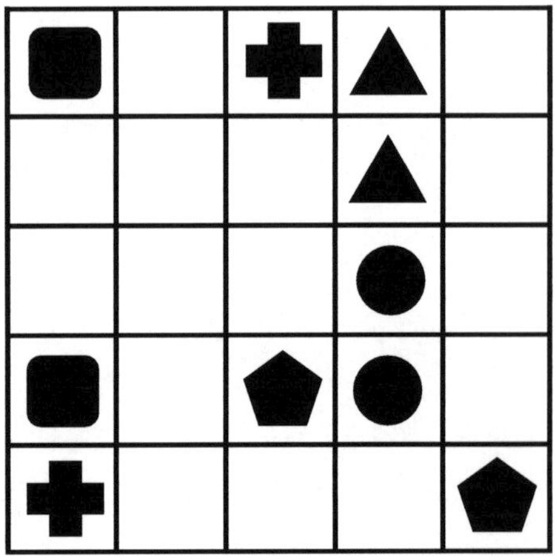

B)

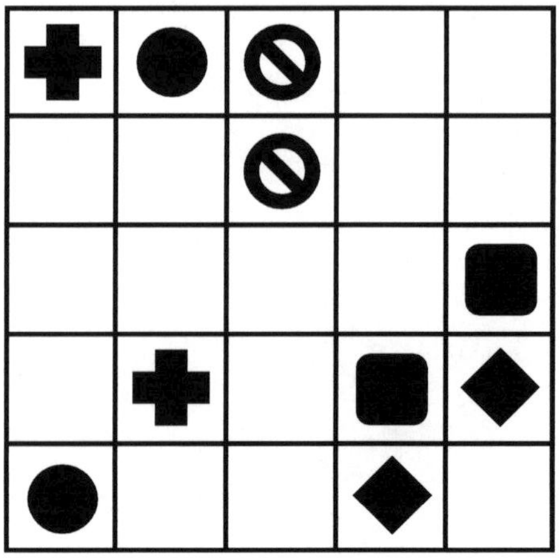

C)

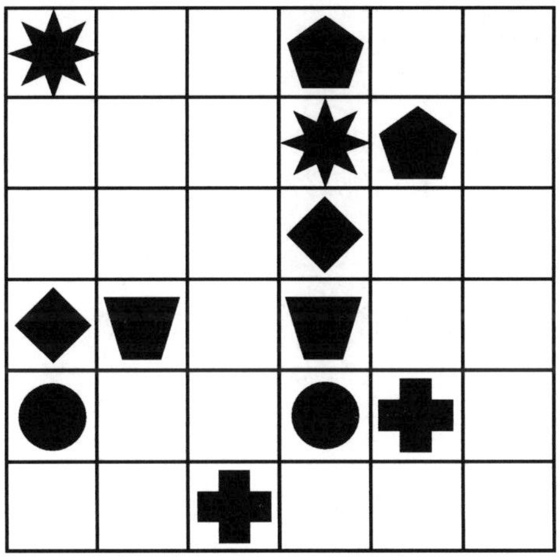

D)

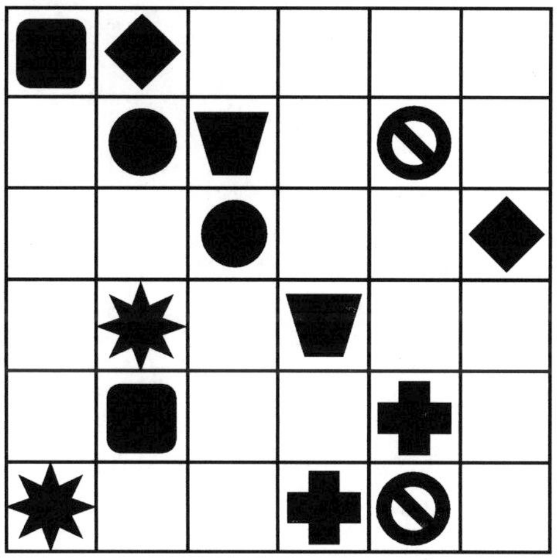

By solving the pairs which have only one way to work, you can make solving the longer and more complex ones easier

E)

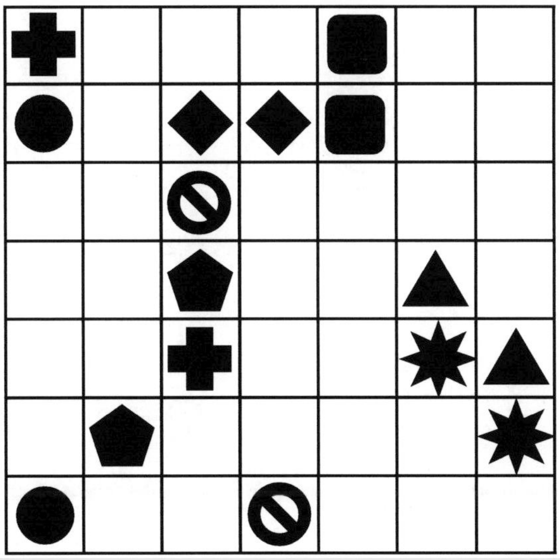

F)

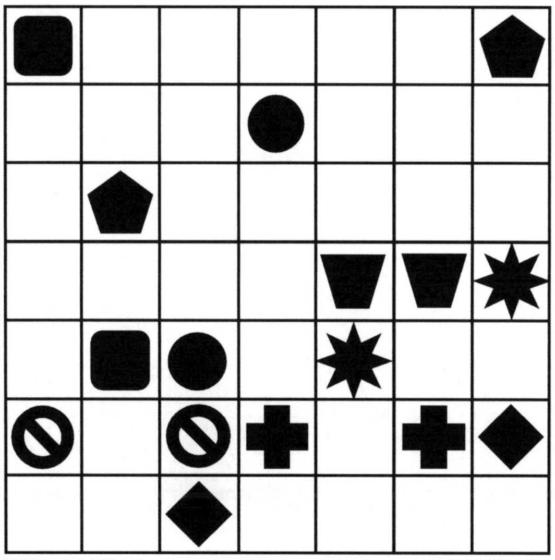

# 11. Killer Sudoku

**Killer Sudoku is just like normal sudoku, but with a twist: there are also smaller boxes which add up to different numbers, indicated by the smaller numbers.**

**The Rules**

- You can use 1-4, or 1-6 in the 6x6 grids
- No row, column, or grid box can have repeating numbers
- Each dashed box has a clue, which is the total the numbers within that box must add up to

Use the example to help you solve the rest.

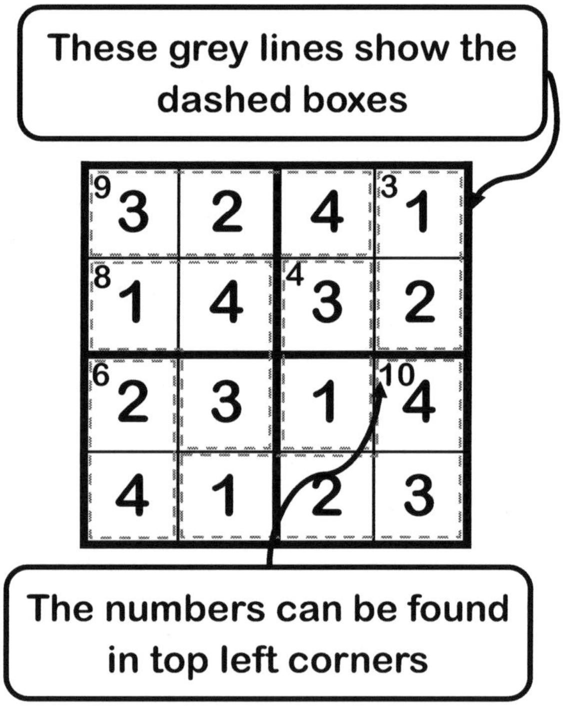


A)

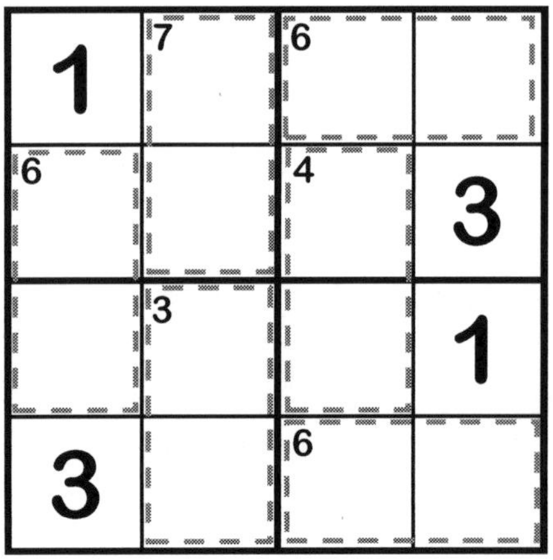

B)

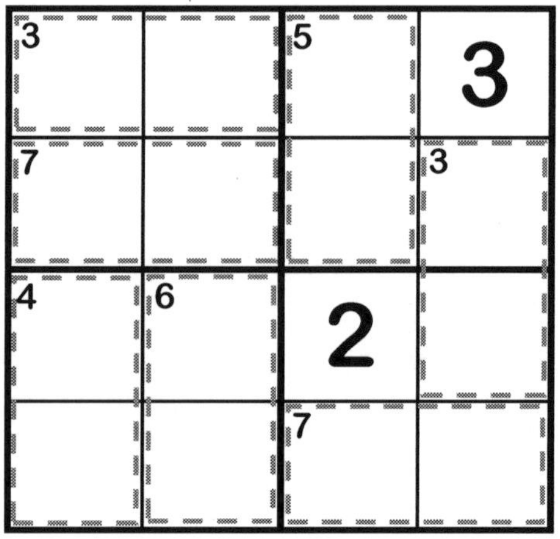

C)

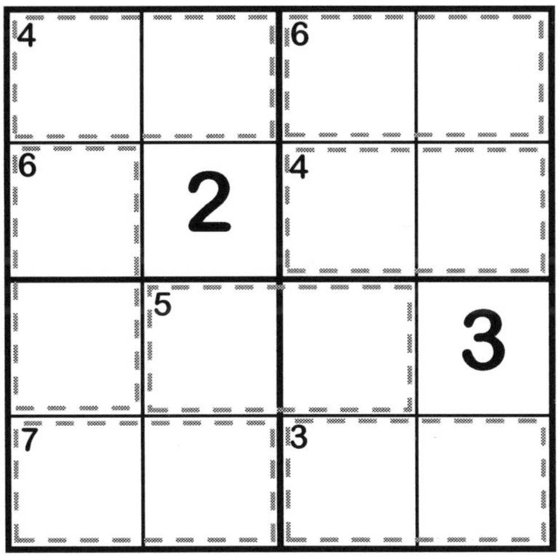

D)

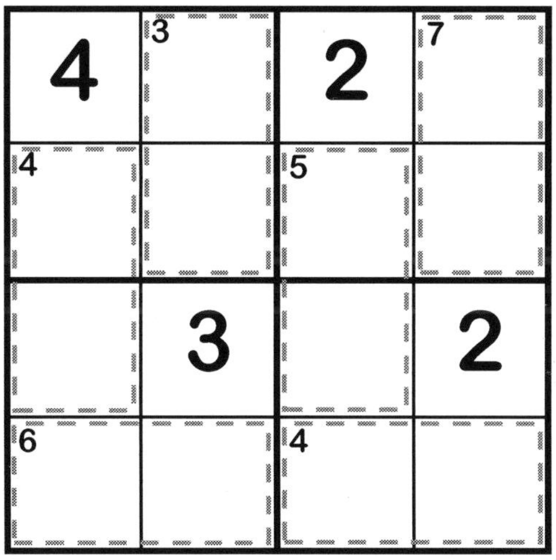

**Try to work out what numbers could go into the marked boxes, and then work out how they could fit together within the puzzle**

E)

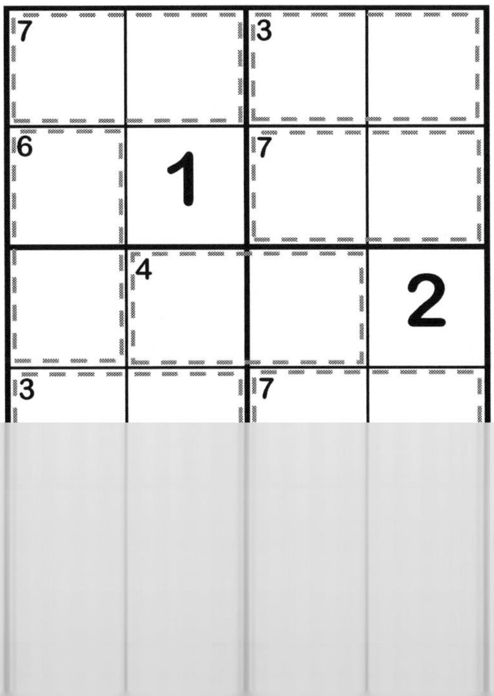

F)

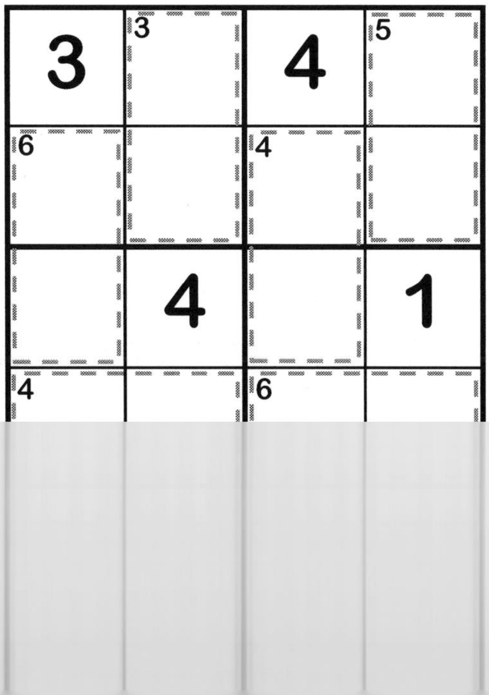

# 12. Numbers Round

**The Rules**

- Using any sum (multiplication, subtraction etc.), create the target number using the smaller numbers
- You can only use each number once, but do not have to use every number

> Sums do not need to be consecutive: you can create two separate sums and combine them later. For example:
>
> 2x2=4, 3+4=7, 7x4 =28

Try your best to solve these puzzles.

Target number

A)

| 284 | | |
|---|---|---|
| 100 | 10 | 4 |
| 2 | 10 | 4 |

B)

| 154 | | |
|---|---|---|
| 10 | 1 | 5 |
| 3 | 2 | 1 |

C)

| 263 | | |
|---|---|---|
| 25 | 8 | 7 |
| 4 | 1 | 3 |

D)

| 351 | | |
|---|---|---|
| 100 | 2 | 5 |
| 4 | 6 | 7 |

E)

| 588 | | |
|---|---|---|
| 50 | 4 | 7 |
| 5 | 6 | 6 |

F)

| 731 | | |
|---|---|---|
| 50 | 2 | 10 |
| 1 | 7 | 9 |

# 13. Looper

Can you draw the right shapes to fill in these puzzles?

**The Rules**

- Each numbered square shows how many squares must be in that shape
- Each numbered square must be in its own shape
- The rooms can be any shape, as long as they are the right size

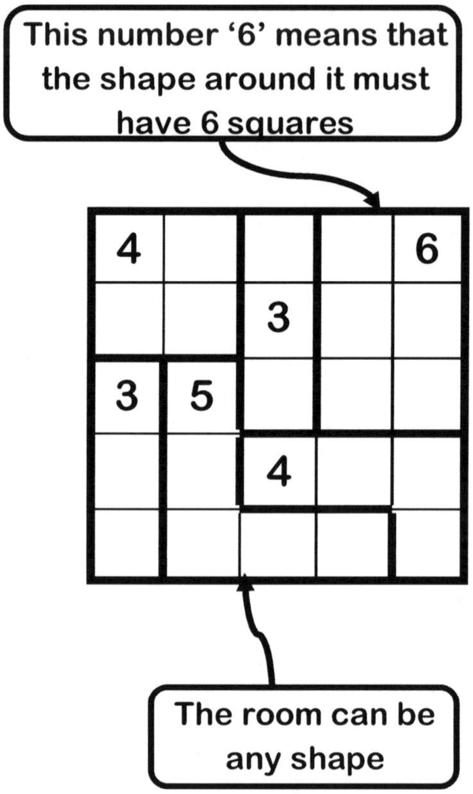


Use the example to help you solve the other puzzles

A)

| | | | |
|---|---|---|---|
| 3 | | | |
| 4 | | 2 | |
| | | | |
| 3 | | | 4 |

B)

| | | | |
|---|---|---|---|
| | | 3 | |
| | | | |
| 3 | | 4 | |
| 2 | | 4 | |

C)

| | | | | |
|---|---|---|---|---|
| | | 4 | | |
| | | 5 | | |
| 3 | | 3 | | |
| 4 | | 6 | | |
| | | | | |

D)

| | | | | |
|---|---|---|---|---|
| 3 | | | | |
| 4 | 4 | | 4 | |
| | | | 5 | |
| | 3 | | | |
| | | | 2 | |

E)

| | | | | | |
|---|---|---|---|---|---|
| | | | | | |
| | 4 | 4 | | | 3 |
| | 4 | | | 4 | |
| | 4 | 6 | | | |
| | | | | | 3 |
| | | 4 | | | |

F)

| | | | | | |
|---|---|---|---|---|---|
| 3 | | | 3 | | 6 |
| | | | | | |
| | 6 | | | | |
| 4 | | 4 | | | |
| | | | | | 4 |
| 6 | | | | | |

# 14. Beehive Hidato

Can you fill in the grids, forming a sequence from the lowest to the highest number?

## The Rules

- Each number must be connected in sequence
- The sequence must include each number already in the grids

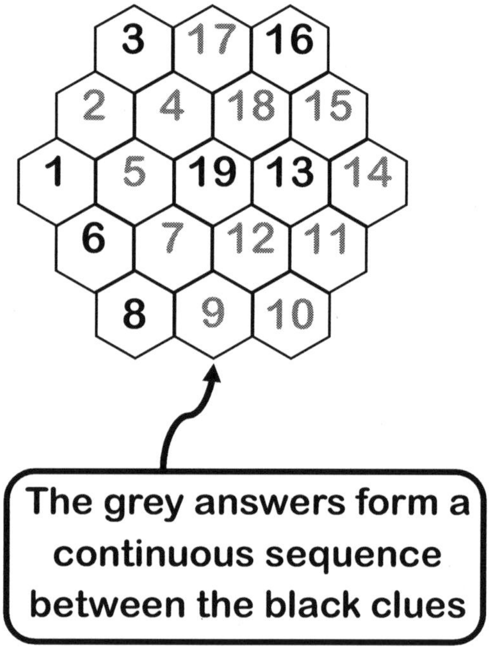


Try your best to solve these puzzles, using the example as a guide.

A)

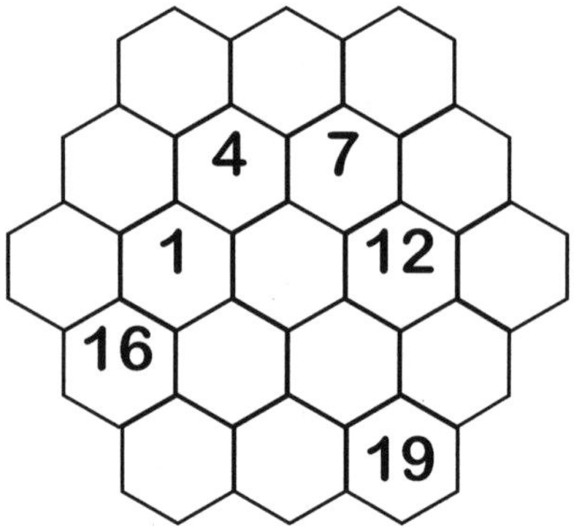


B)

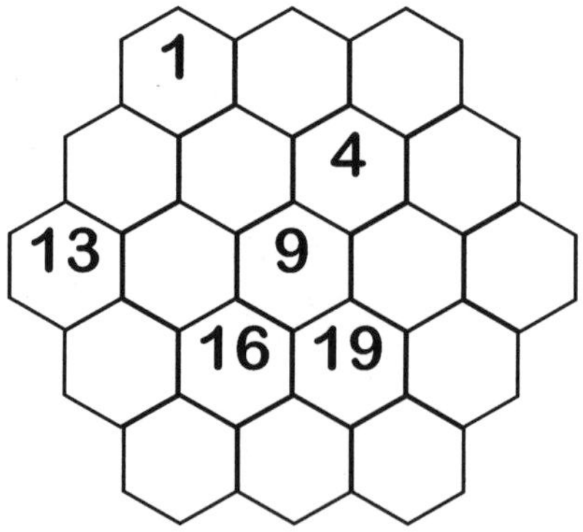

C)

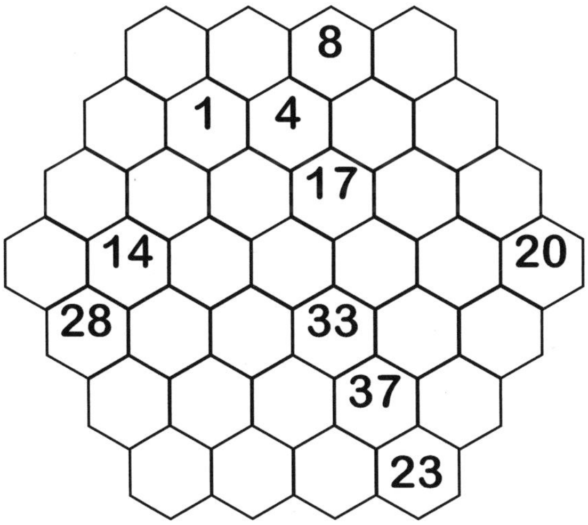
8
1
4
17
14
20
28
33
37
23

D)

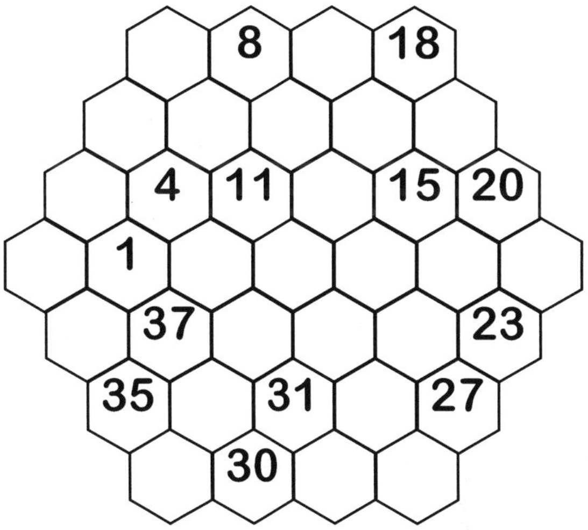
8
18
4
11
15
20
1
37
23
35
31
27
30

E)

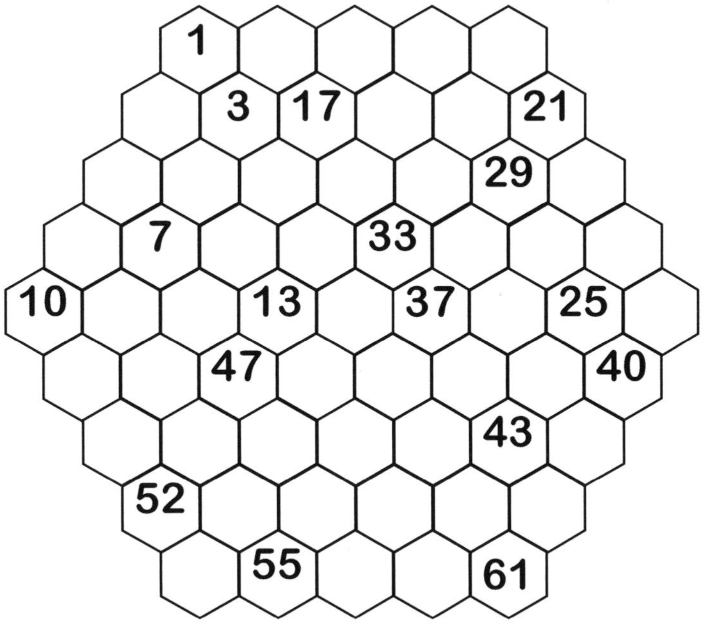
1
3
17
21
29
7
33
10
13
37
25
47
40
43
52
55
61

# 15. Suko

**Suko is a challenging game of addition. Can you follow the rules and fill in the grid?**

**<u>The Rules</u>**

- **Each grid must be filled 1-9, with no repeated numbers**
- **Each circled number shows the sum of the numbers around it**

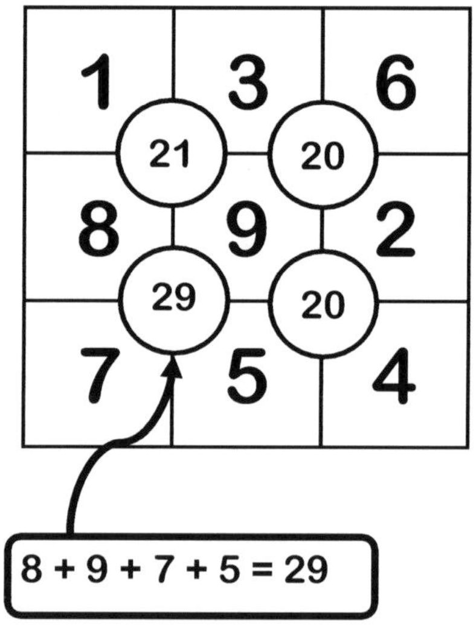


**Try your best to solve these puzzles, using the example as a guide.**

**A)**

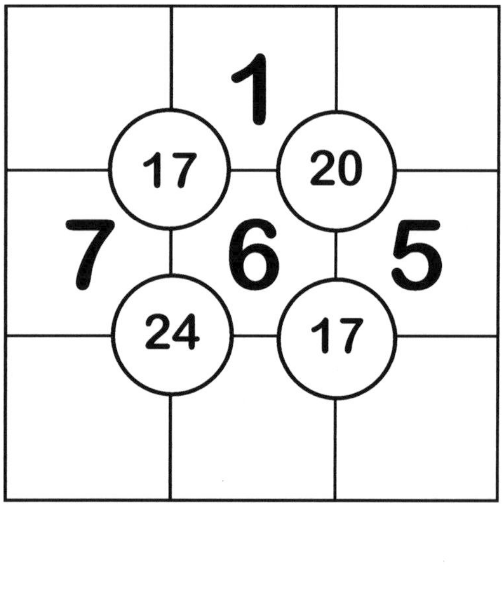


**B)**

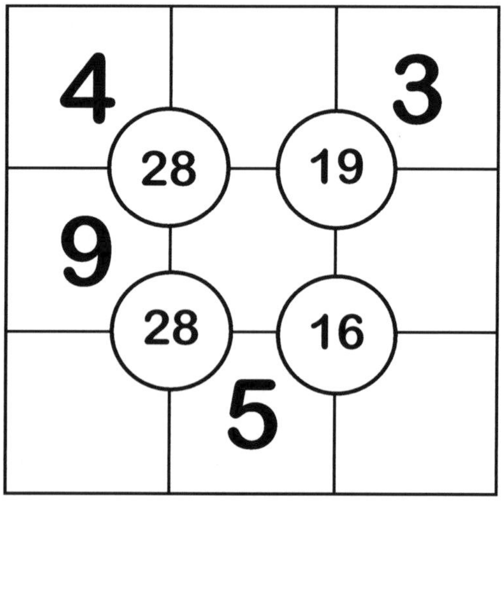

C)

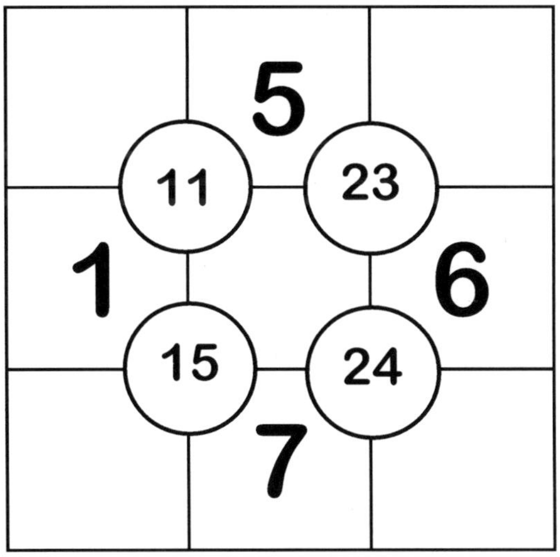


D)

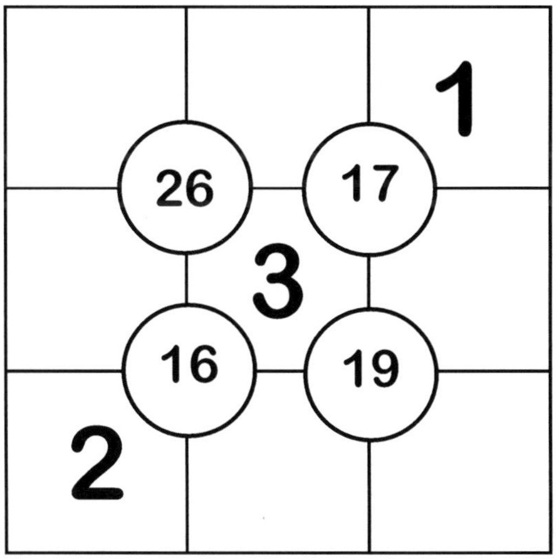


E)

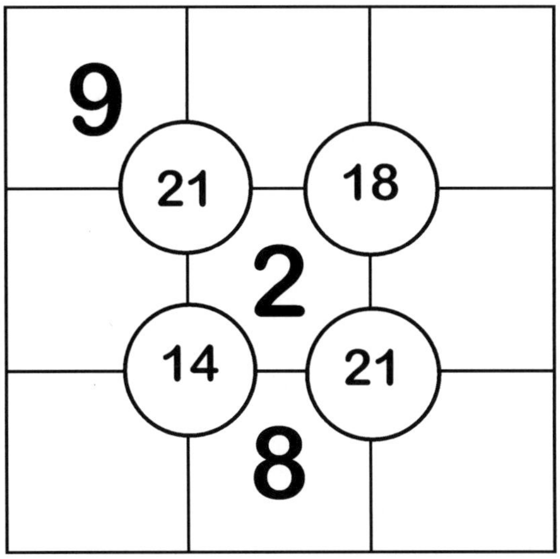


F)

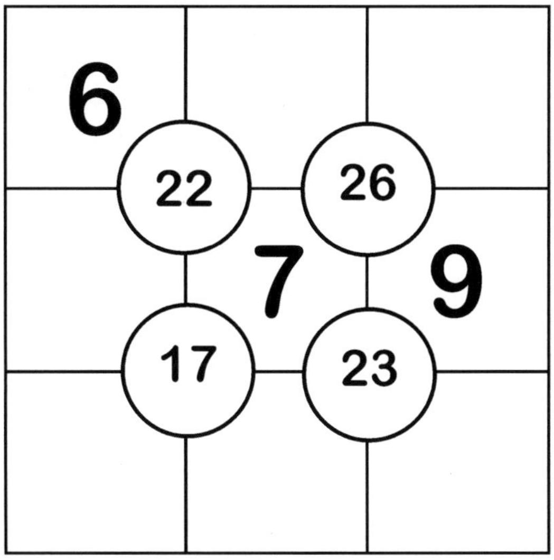

# 16. Quick Calcs

Can you follow these functions for a quick mental calculation challenge? Follow these sums along, and try to do them all in your head for an extra challenge.

A)

| | | |
|---|---|---|
| 1 | 2 | 3 |
| +7 | x4 | x10 |
| +9 | +17 | -7 |
| +21 | +7 | +22 |
| -17 | +21 | -19 |
| = | = | = |

B)

| | | |
|---|---|---|
| 2 | 4 | 6 |
| x9 | x4 | x10 |
| +12 | x2 | -7 |
| ÷2 | +8 | +22 |
| +7 | -20 | -19 |
| = | = | = |

C)

| | | |
|---|---|---|
| 3 | 5 | 10 |
| x3 | x8 | x8 |
| x3 | +20 | +25 |
| +33 | -17 | -31 |
| -3 | -23 | -19 |
| = | = | = |

D)

| | | |
|---|---|---|
| 4 | 8 | 12 |
| x3 | x6 | x10 |
| x3 | x2 | +30 |
| +17 | +4 | ÷5 |
| +21 | ÷25 | x2 |
| = | = | = |

E)

| | | |
|---|---|---|
| 5 | 10 | 15 |
| x5 | x3 | x3 |
| x3 | x3 | +5 |
| x5 | -50 | x10 |
| x2 | ÷2 | -101 |
| = | = | = |

# 17. Sequences

**Each of these sequences has a pattern between the numbers. Can you find it and work out the next two answers in the sequence?**

**A): 1 2 3 4 … …**

**0 2 4 6 … …**

**1 2 4 8 … …**

**B): 1 3 6 10 … …**

**1 4 7 10 … …**

**1 3 7 13 … …**

C): 5 4 6 5 … …

20 18 15 11 … …

2 3 5 9 … …

D): A B C D … …

A C E G … …

V U S P … …

E): A B D H … …

K J L I … …

MN NO OP PQ … …

# 18. Wordmills

Can you find the right pairs, and fill in these puzzles?

## The Rules

- Each puzzle has central letters, which form words with two of the other pairs (so a central SD could combine with WI and OM to make WI SD OM)

Try your best to solve these challenging wordmills.

A)

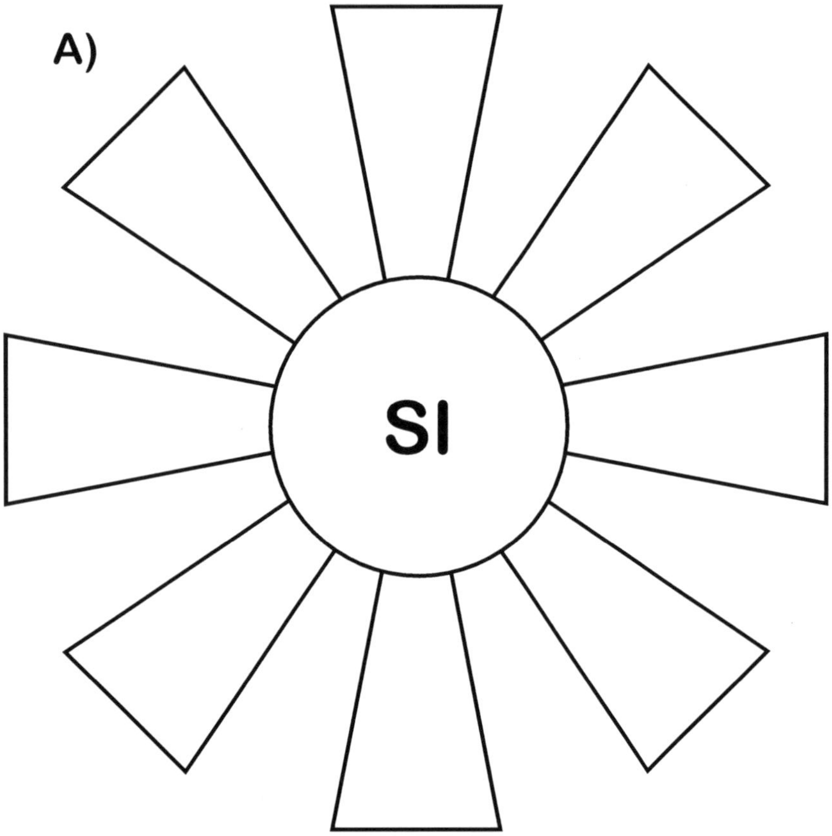


| | |
|---|---|
| DE | DE |
| DE | BE |
| RI | IN |
| GN | NG |

B)

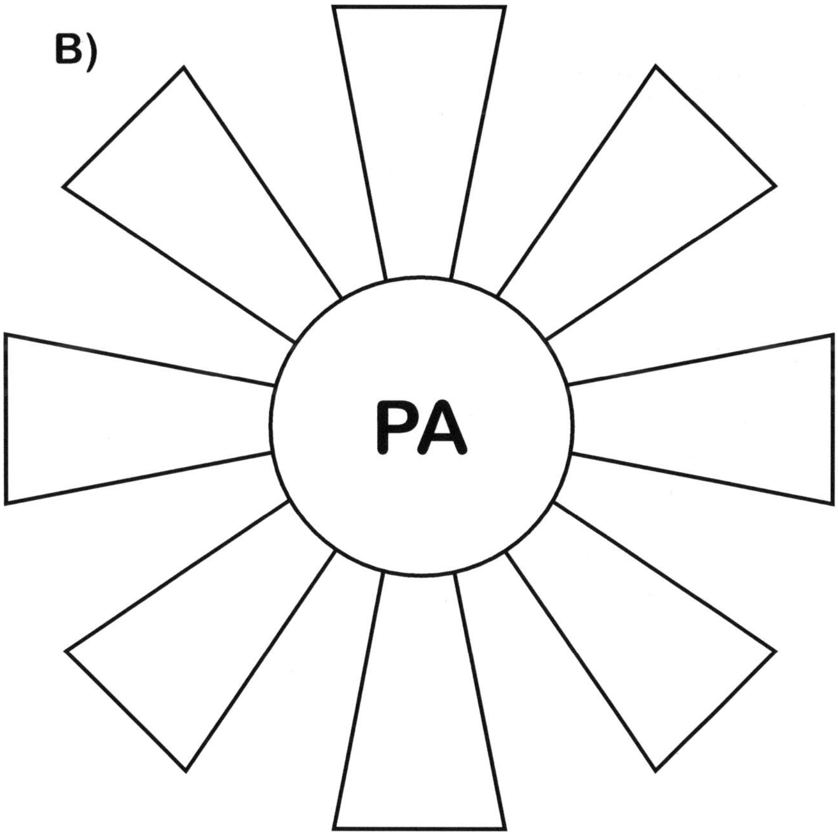


| | |
|---|---|
| EX | IR |
| IM | DE |
| RT | ND |
| CT | RE |

C)

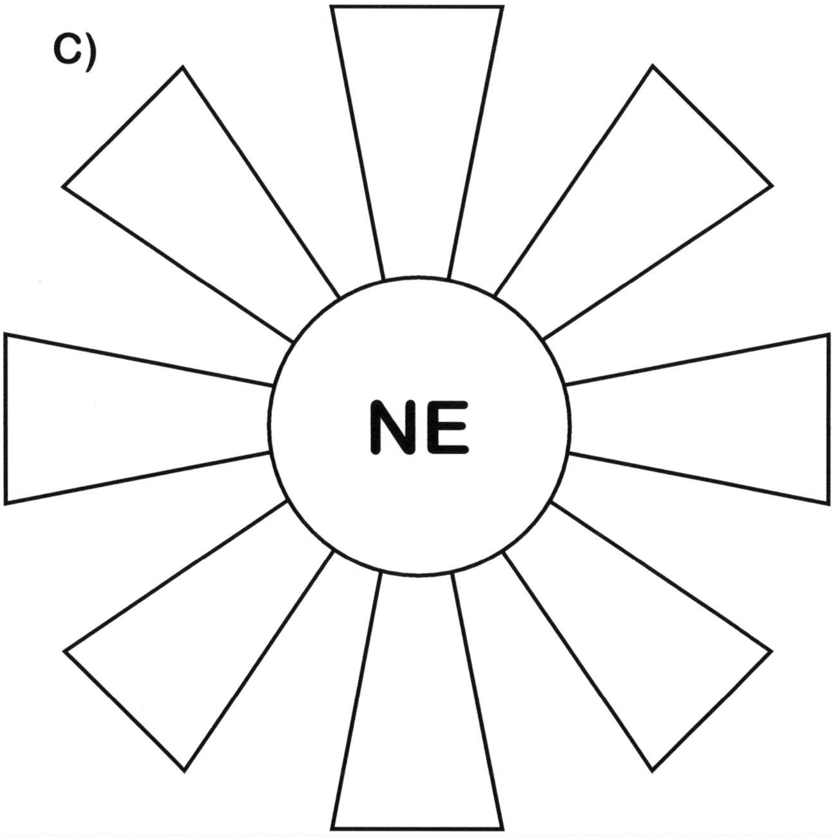


| | |
|---|---|
| LY | CI |
| TY | ST |
| HO | MA |
| NI | LO |

# 19. Across Down

Can you solve the sums, and fill in the puzzle grid?

**The Rules**

- Each grid must be filled in so all sums are correct
- Each number already in is correct, and provide clues to help you

Any numbers can be used in these grids, as longs as the sums are correct

Try your best to solve these puzzles

A)

| | | | | |
|---|---|---|---|---|
| 7 | + | | = | |
| + | | + | | + |
| | + | | = | 11 |
| = | | = | | = |
| 15 | + | 12 | = | |

B)

| | | | | |
|---|---|---|---|---|
| | + | 14 | = | |
| + | | + | | + |
| 19 | + | | = | 23 |
| = | | = | | = |
| 31 | + | | = | |

C)

| | | | | | | |
|---|---|---|---|---|---|---|
| 2 | + | 7 | + | 9 | = | |
| + | | + | | + | | + |
| | + | 4 | + | | = | 18 |
| + | | + | | + | | + |
| 5 | + | | + | 4 | = | |
| = | | = | | = | | = |
| 10 | + | 18 | + | | = | |

D)

| | | | | | | |
|---|---|---|---|---|---|---|
| | + | 9 | + | | = | 21 |
| + | | + | | + | | + |
| 7 | + | | + | 7 | = | 20 |
| + | | + | | + | | + |
| 10 | + | | + | | = | 20 |
| = | | = | | = | | = |
| | + | 16 | + | 20 | = | |

E)

| | | | | | | |
|---|---|---|---|---|---|---|
| 7 | + | | + | 6 | = | |
| + | | - | | - | | |
| | + | 1 | + | | = | 7 |
| - | | x | | + | | |
| 2 | x | | - | 3 | = | 3 |
| = | | = | | = | | |
| 9 | | 12 | | 7 | | |

F)

| | | | | | | |
|---|---|---|---|---|---|---|
| | - | 3 | + | | = | 17 |
| + | | + | | + | | |
| | + | | - | 17 | = | 15 |
| - | | ÷ | | - | | |
| 7 | - | | + | 13 | = | 16 |
| = | | = | | = | | |
| | | 6 | | 16 | | |

# 20. Hidden Code

**Can you cross out one letter from each pair to spell out a joke?**

**Each separate block makes its own word.**

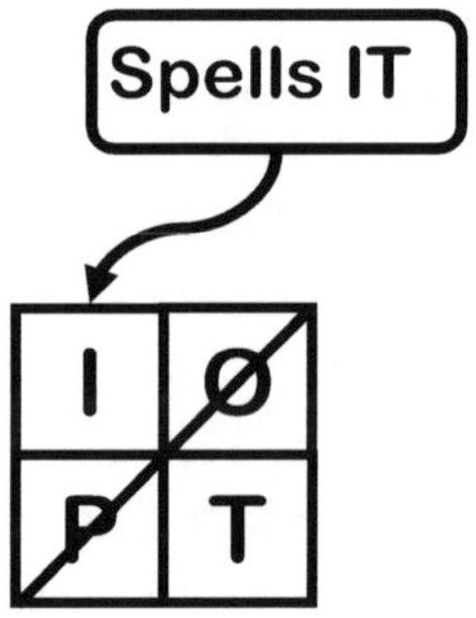


A)

| | | | |
|---|---|---|---|
| W | E | A | T |
| R | H | L | I |

| | |
|---|---|
| D | Y |
| T | O |

| | | |
|---|---|---|
| B | E | U |
| Y | O | N |

| | | |
|---|---|---|
| D | E | I |
| G | S | T |

| | |
|---|---|
| M | E |
| I | F |

| | | |
|---|---|---|
| Y | N | T |
| I | O | U |

| | | | | |
|---|---|---|---|---|
| C | A | C | S | S |
| O | R | O | O | N |

| |
|---|
| A |
| S |

| | | | | | | |
|---|---|---|---|---|---|---|
| S | N | U | W | T | A | H |
| T | R | O | C | M | T | N |

| | | |
|---|---|---|
| A | I | C |
| T | N | D |

| |
|---|
| N |
| A |

| | | | | | | |
|---|---|---|---|---|---|---|
| V | O | T | P | I | T | E |
| N | A | M | F | A | R | H |

?

| | | | | | | | | |
|---|---|---|---|---|---|---|---|---|
| F | M | O | S | T | I | N | T | E |
| O | R | S | A | V | B | I | G | C |

B)

| | | | |
|---|---|---|---|
| W | H | K | T |
| S | I | A | E |

| | | | |
|---|---|---|---|
| K | H | A | D |
| T | I | N | T |

| | |
|---|---|
| S | T |
| O | F |

| | | | | |
|---|---|---|---|---|
| H | E | O | R | S |
| S | H | W | E | O |

| | |
|---|---|
| D | G |
| N | O |

| | | | | | |
|---|---|---|---|---|---|
| N | I | B | E | A | W |
| U | M | N | J | R | S |

| | | | |
|---|---|---|---|
| W | I | E | R |
| H | E | A | N |

?

| | | | | | | | |
|---|---|---|---|---|---|---|---|
| S | N | F | C | E | E | O | S |
| E | R | E | A | K | B | R | Y |

C)

| | | | |
|---|---|---|---|
| W | H | H | E |
| I | F | A | T |

| | | | | | |
|---|---|---|---|---|---|
| W | C | R | O | O | N |
| S | E | H | E | A | L |

| | | | | | | |
|---|---|---|---|---|---|---|
| S | U | I | J | G | E | T |
| Y | B | B | G | E | C | R |

| | |
|---|---|
| D | E |
| H | O |

| | | | | | | |
|---|---|---|---|---|---|---|
| W | I | L | C | H | M | Y |
| O | U | T | D | B | E | S |

| | | | |
|---|---|---|---|
| L | I | K | T |
| U | B | R | E |

| | | | |
|---|---|---|---|
| T | E | S | C |
| B | R | I | T |

?

| | | | | | | | |
|---|---|---|---|---|---|---|---|
| S | P | T | D | L | N | D | G |
| U | [illegible] | E | [illegible] | [illegible] | [illegible] | N | [illegible] |

# 21. Crossword

**Can you solve the clues below, and fill in these tricky crossword puzzles?**

**A)**

**ACROSS**

1) A board game with kings and queens
4) A building which goes across a river or gap
5) A large bird, bald or golden
7) Electronic device for accessing the internet
8) A device for taking pictures
9) Someone who looks after sheep

**DOWN**

2) A greyish, expensive metal
3) A large, flying vehicle
6) Plays a role in a movie
10) An instrument that is played by pressing keys

B)

**ACROSS**

1) Uses hands to tell the time

3) A time of year, like Summer and Autumn

4) A round shape

8) A spiky yellow fruit usually cut into rings

9) The largest bodies of water

10) Tool used with nails

**DOWN**

2) A brown, sweet treat

5) A dangerous feature of a river, formed when water flows over a cliff

6) Used for tasting: found in your mouth

7) A piece of glass that you look through

# 22. Wordplay

**Each of these puzzles shows a well known phrase. Can you decipher them all?**

A)

B)

C)

D)

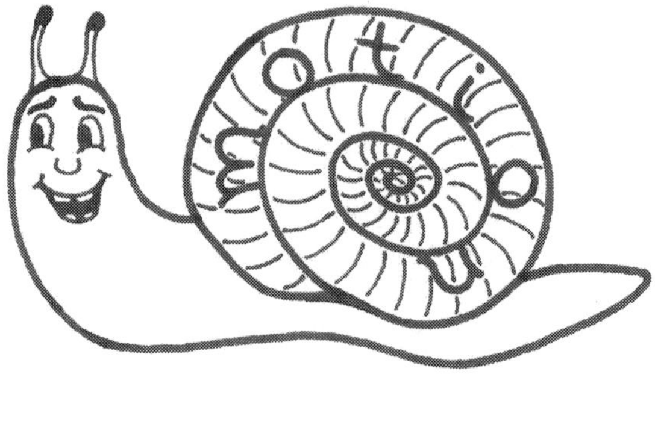

E)

F)

G)

H)

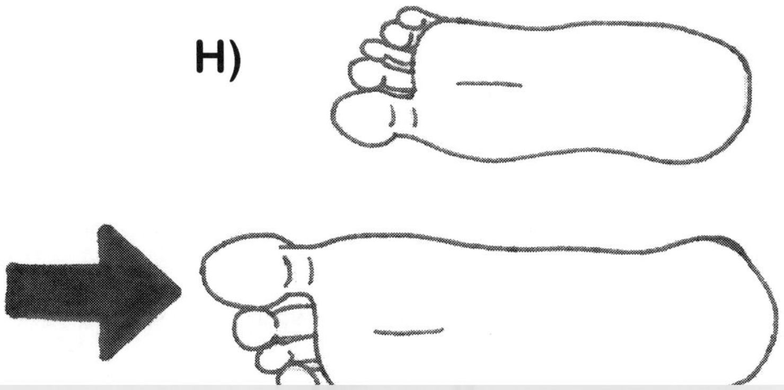

# 23. Codewords

**In these puzzles, each letter has been replaced with a number. Can you crack the code, and fill in these crossword-based puzzles?**

**These clues are all Olympic events...**

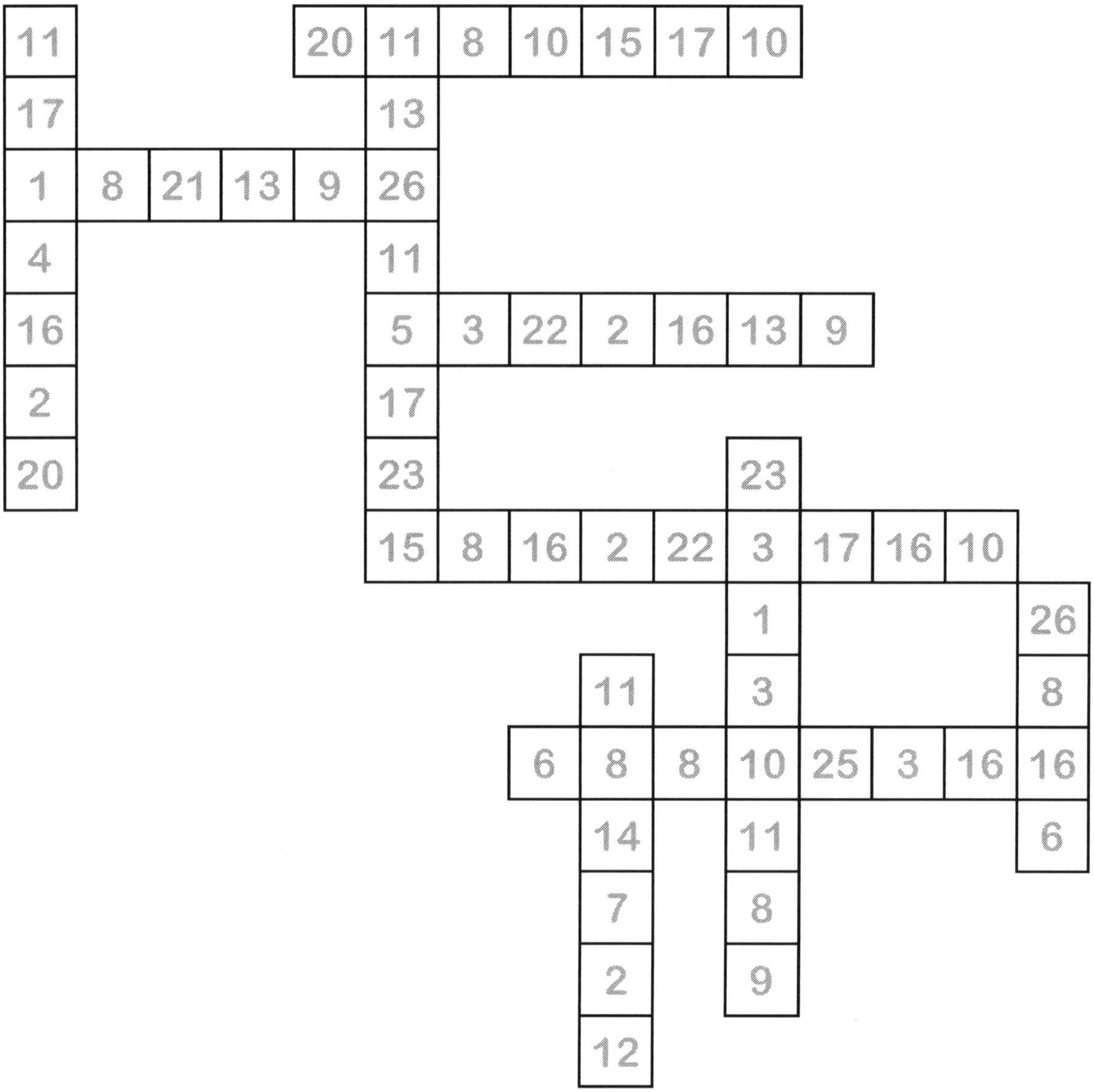


| | | | | | | | | | | | | |
|---|---|---|---|---|---|---|---|---|---|---|---|---|
| 1: | 2: | 3: | 4: D | 5: J | 6: F | 7: | 8: O | 9: | 10: | 11: | 12: | 13: |
| 14: | 15: | 16: | 17: | 18: X | 19: Q | 20: | 21: | 22: | 23: | 24: Z | 25: | 26: |

...while these are all animals.

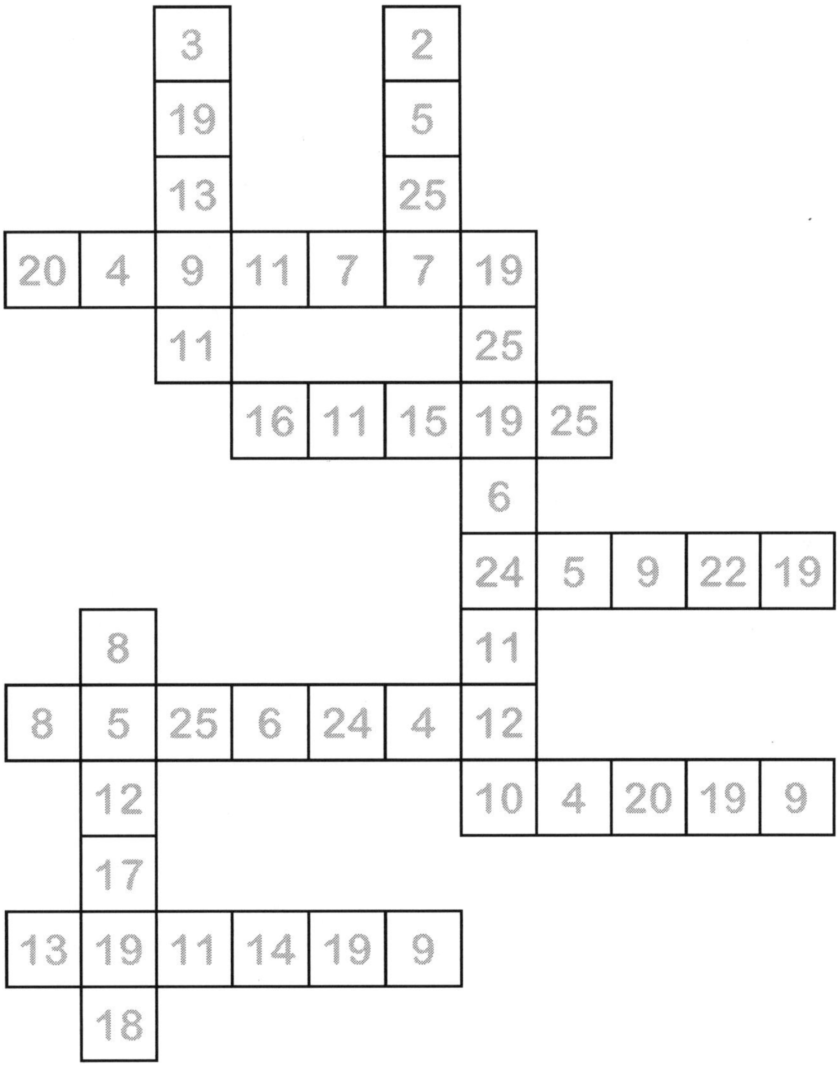


| | | | | | | | | | | | | |
|---|---|---|---|---|---|---|---|---|---|---|---|---|
| 1: Q | 2: W | 3: | 4: | 5: | 6: P | 7: F | 8: | 9: | 10: | 11: A | 12: | 13: B |
| 14: | 15: | 16: | 17: | 18: | 19: | 20: | 21: J | 22: | 23: U | 24: | 25: | 26: X |

# 24. Building Bridges

Can you bridge the gap in these puzzles?

**The Rules:**

- Each island must be connect to the rest by bridges
- Each island has a number, and that indicates the exact number of bridges to that island
- A bridge cannot be diagonal, and must be straight

Use the example to help you attempt the rest of the puzzles.

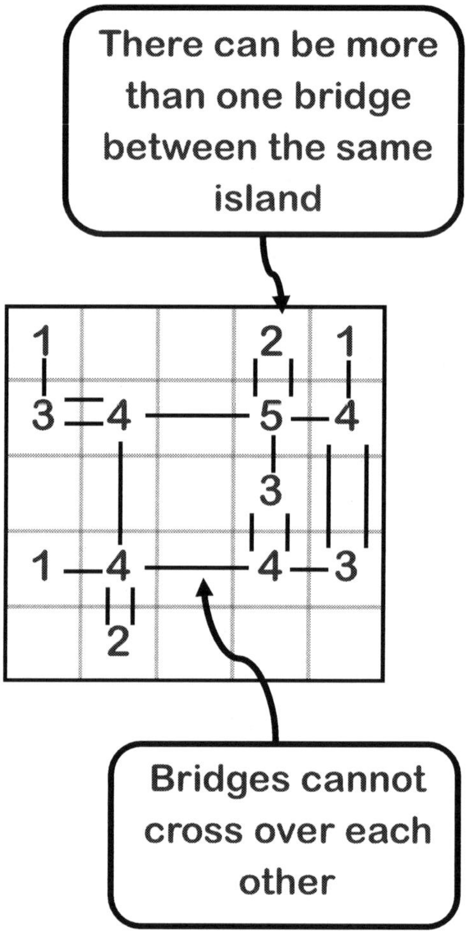


A)

| | | | |
|---|---|---|---|
| 1 | | 1 | |
| 3 | | 2 | |
| | | | 1 |
| 2 | | | 2 |

B)

| | | | |
|---|---|---|---|
| 2 | 3 | | 1 |
| | 4 | | 2 |
| | | | 1 |
| 2 | 3 | | 2 |

C)

| | | | | |
|---|---|---|---|---|
| | 3 | | 1 | |
| | 4 | 4 | | 3 |
| | | 1 | | 1 |
| 2 | 3 | | 1 | |
| 1 | | | | |

D)

| | | | | |
|---|---|---|---|---|
| 1 | | | | |
| | | | 1 | 2 |
| 3 | | 1 | | 3 |
| | | 1 | | |
| 5 | | 5 | | 2 |

**By solving the islands which only have one option, it may make it easier to solve the more open islands**

E)

| | | | | | |
|---|---|---|---|---|---|
| 2 | 1 | | | | |
| | | | 2 | | 1 |
| 4 | | | 4 | | 1 |
| | | 1 | 3 | | 1 |
| 3 | 2 | | | | |
| | 1 | | | | |

F)

| | | | | | |
|---|---|---|---|---|---|
| 1 | 4 | | 2 | | |
| | | | 2 | | 1 |
| 1 | 4 | | | | |
| | | | | | |
| | | | 2 | 2 | |
| | 3 | | 3 | 1 | |

# 25. The Wall

Can you sort these walls of answers into groups of four,

Each group has a common theme, and some answers may fit into more than one group, but will only make a group of four in one of them

| | | | |
|---|---|---|---|
| KITTEN | OWL | OSTRICH | TIN |
| PUPPY | BEJING | IRON | CUB |
| COPPER | BANGKOK | ATHENS | LEAD |
| KID | PARIS | EAGLE | PELICAN |

1. ..............................................................

..............................................................

2. ..............................................................

..............................................................

3. ..............................................................

..............................................................

4. ..............................................................

..............................................................

| | | | |
|---|---|---|---|
| EVEREST | THAMES | LOCUST | WASP |
| MOSQUITO | AMAZON | BLANC | WILLOW |
| REDWOOD | K2 | PINE | BUTTERFLY |
| OAK | NILE | MISSISSIPPI | FUJI |

1. ........................................................
........................................................

2. ........................................................
........................................................

3. ........................................................
........................................................

4. ........................................................
........................................................

| | | | |
|---|---|---|---|
| GREEK | LARGE | OWT | EERHT |
| SEA | ROMAN | ENO | MASSIVE |
| EGYPTIAN | GIANT | PEA | RUOF |
| TEA | HUGE | AZTEC | BEE |

1. ........................................................
........................................................

2. ........................................................
........................................................

# 26. Times Square

**Can you multiply your way out of these problems to solve the puzzles?**

**<u>The Rules:</u>**

- **In this puzzle, you must place the numbers 1-4, 1-5, or 1-6 as the grids get bigger**
- **Numbers cannot be repeated in any row or column**
- **The numbers within each smaller block must multiply to make the target number**

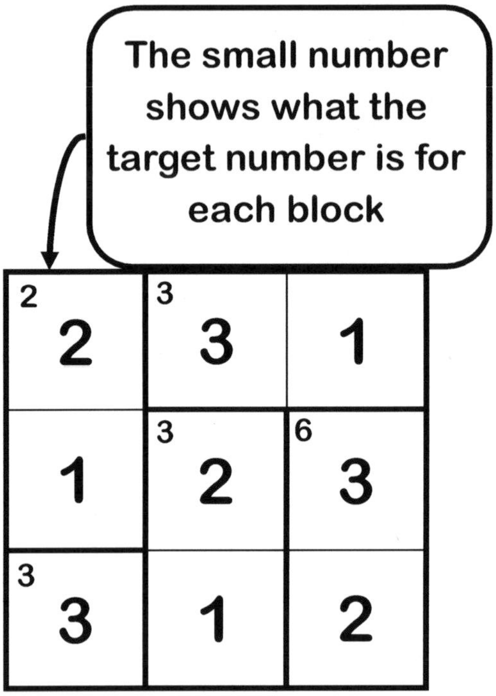


**A)**

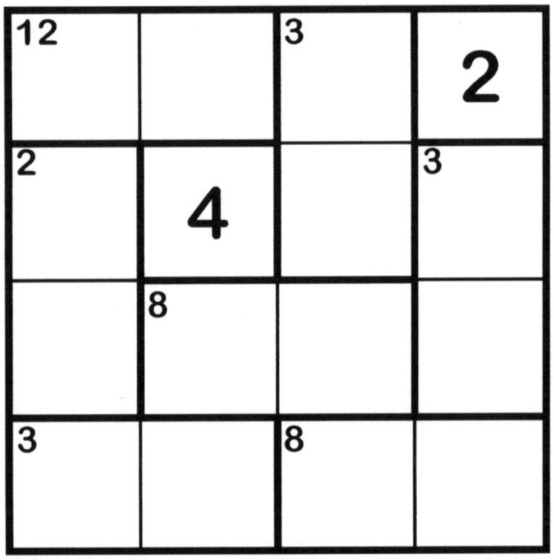


**B)**

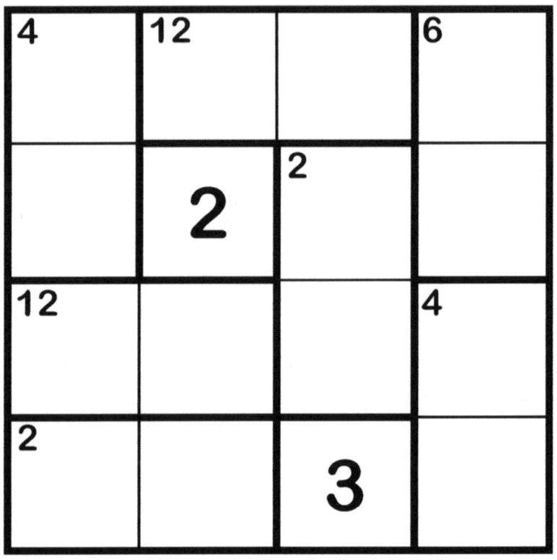

C)

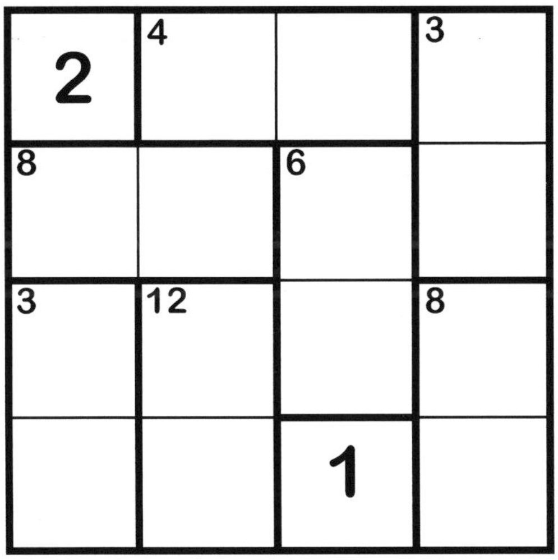


D)

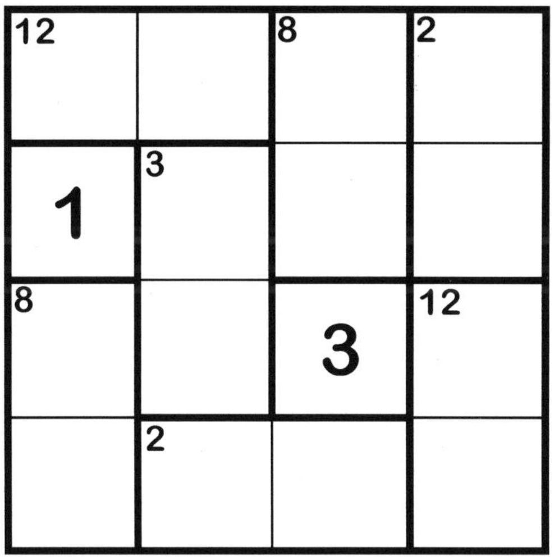


By solving which numbers are in which boxes, it will become easier to decide which way around they should be compared to the others

E)

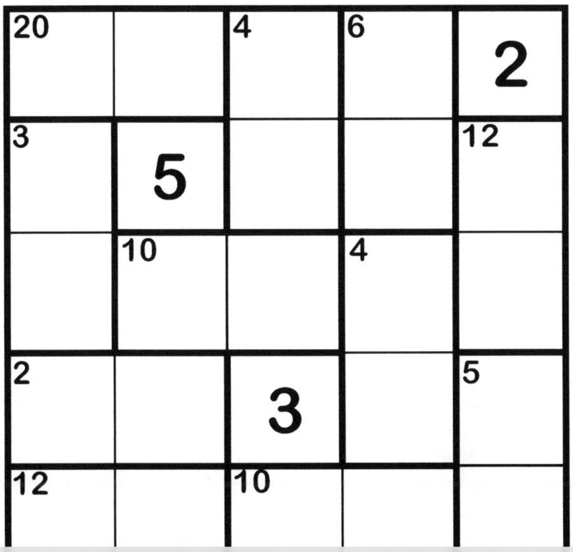


F)

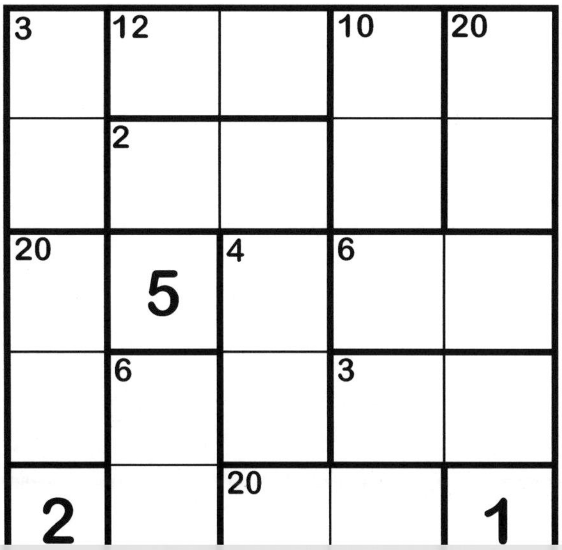

# 27. Wordsearch

## Countries

| | | | | | | | | | | | | | | |
|---|---|---|---|---|---|---|---|---|---|---|---|---|---|---|
| C | R | I | U | A | Y | A | S | I | H | O | N | L | A | W |
| S | A | K | N | L | U | O | C | P | N | F | I | R | I | A |
| A | Q | N | A | D | Y | S | O | I | Y | S | A | S | B | P |
| K | C | T | A | K | I | D | T | D | R | E | P | U | I | O |
| G | I | G | P | D | N | A | L | R | S | E | S | F | M | G |
| R | F | X | U | A | A | Q | A | X | A | E | M | L | A | M |
| R | U | M | L | F | B | X | N | Z | V | L | L | A | N | E |
| P | V | G | I | R | O | K | D | P | J | O | I | A | O | X |
| Z | N | J | A | Y | Y | N | A | M | R | E | G | A | W | I |
| E | I | Z | B | L | K | K | A | I | B | M | A | Z | C | C |
| T | I | W | Z | I | I | K | E | N | Y | A | M | E | H | O |
| L | T | E | W | S | M | R | B | I | C | C | F | Y | I | G |
| S | W | I | T | Z | E | R | L | A | N | D | S | N | N | X |
| F | R | A | N | C | E | D | B | J | S | P | E | U | A | H |
| O | N | M | R | T | E | V | J | U | Y | A | O | E | F | J |

| | | | |
|---|---|---|---|
| AMERICA | ENGLAND | ITALY | SCOTLAND |
| AUSTRALIA | FIJI | KENYA | SPAIN |
| BRAZIL | FRANCE | MEXICO | SWITZERLAND |
| CANADA | GERMANY | NAMIBIA | WALES |
| CHINA | INDIA | PAKISTAN | ZAMBIA |

# Cities

| | | | | | | | | | | | | | | |
|---|---|---|---|---|---|---|---|---|---|---|---|---|---|---|
| C | Q | O | M | M | K | J | L | K | A | Q | R | W | G | I |
| O | T | I | U | Q | L | F | A | R | A | V | W | N | W | B |
| S | G | N | R | H | N | O | C | K | J | B | I | J | F | N |
| W | Z | F | Z | A | X | M | H | O | A | J | U | I | B | C |
| D | I | R | D | A | M | X | M | K | I | R | R | L | N | D |
| H | G | R | U | B | N | I | D | E | C | J | T | F | B | J |
| C | A | R | D | I | F | F | B | K | I | O | K | A | E | W |
| C | A | I | R | O | B | C | U | C | K | W | T | D | R | U |
| O | C | E | F | E | F | W | K | P | N | A | T | S | L | O |
| A | X | R | R | O | L | M | A | D | I | N | V | A | I | R |
| I | W | G | W | O | S | I | B | K | S | N | G | K | N | P |
| D | A | A | N | D | O | N | F | D | L | E | K | L | A | E |
| Z | Y | D | T | V | T | S | J | N | E | I | L | R | M | C |
| B | O | S | N | T | K | K | U | S | H | V | I | O | C | B |
| N | S | D | H | I | O | P | X | B | W | S | R | M | S | F |

| | | | |
|---|---|---|---|
| BAKU | EDINBURGH | MADRID | ROME |
| BEIJING | HELSINKI | MINSK | SOFIA |
| BERLIN | JAKARTA | OTTAWA | STOCKHOLM |
| CAIRO | KABUL | PARIS | VIENNA |
| CARDIFF | LONDON | QUITO | ZAGREB |

# 28. Riddles

Can you solve these challenging brain teasers?

A) What goes up and down stairs without moving?

B) What goes up when the rain comes down?

C) What has hands, but cannot clap?

D) What do you call a boomerang that doesn't come back?

E) What goes through towns, and over hills, but never moves?

F) I go around the yard, but never move. What am I?

G) What is always coming, but never arrives?

H) How many birthdays does the average person have?

I) What will an empty hand fill?

J) What can you put through glass without shattering it?

K) What is full of holes, but still holds water?

L) What can you blow up, but leave in perfect condition?

M) How can someone be born on Christmas Day, but have their birthday in summer?

N) I have a tongue, but never talk. I have no legs, but I often go for a walk. What am I?

O) You bring me to dinner, but never eat me. What am I?

P) What goes through a door, but never enters or leaves a room?

Q) How can you make a net hold water?

R) What can you hold without ever using your hands?

# 29. Sequence Snake

By placing numbers into these grids, can you complete a line throughout the puzzles?

**The Rules:**

- Each number must be connected in sequence, so that a line can be drawn
- The line cannot cross over itself
- Both 1 and the largest number (16 for 4x4, 25 for 5x5, and 36 for 6x6) are already marked

Try your best to solve these puzzles.

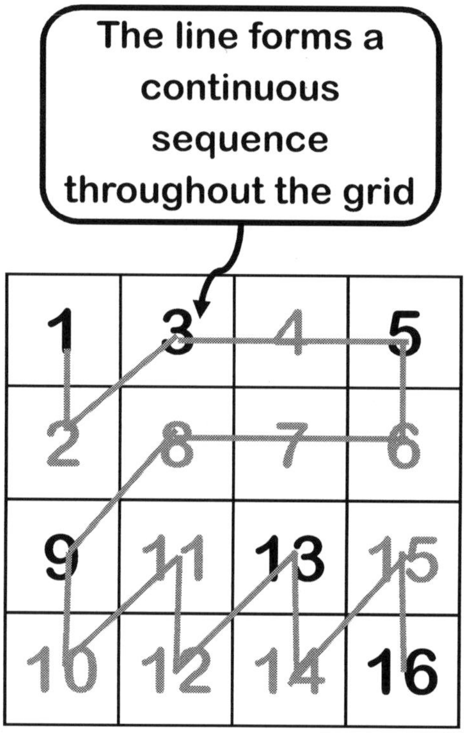


A)

| | | | |
|---|---|---|---|
| | | | |
| 12 | | 8 | |
| | 16 | | 4 |
| | | | 1 |

B)

| | | | |
|---|---|---|---|
| | | 11 | |
| | 7 | 16 | |
| | | | |
| 4 | | | 1 |

C)

| | | | |
|---|---|---|---|
| | | 4 | |
| 1 | | | |
| | 11 | 8 | |
| | | | 16 |

D)

| | | | |
|---|---|---|---|
| 1 | | | 7 |
| | 4 | | |
| | | 16 | |
| 13 | | | 10 |

**Rather than worrying about the entire line, try to solve it to the next number in the sequence, and go from there**

E)

| | | | | |
|---|---|---|---|---|
| | | | 1 | |
| | 25 | | 4 | |
| 21 | | | | 7 |
| | | | 10 | |
| 17 | | | 14 | |

F)

| | | | | |
|---|---|---|---|---|
| 1 | 16 | | | |
| | | | 20 | |
| | | | 12 | |
| 4 | | 8 | | |
| | | | | 25 |

# 30. Windoku

Can you tackle these sudoku puzzles with a twist?

**The Rules:**

- You must place the numbers 1-9 into the grid without repeating numbers in any row, column, or marked box
- Each shaded area must also contain 1-9 with no repeats

Try your best to solve these puzzles

A)

| | | | | | | | | |
|---|---|---|---|---|---|---|---|---|
| 9 | 3 | 8 | 2 | | 6 | | 1 | |
| 1 | | 7 | 9 | | 8 | | 2 | |
| | 5 | 2 | | | 7 | | 3 | 8 |
| 2 | | 3 | | | 1 | 5 | 4 | 7 |
| 7 | | 9 | 4 | | 5 | | 8 | |
| | 8 | 4 | 7 | 2 | | 1 | 6 | 9 |
| 4 | 9 | | | 1 | | | | 6 |
| 8 | 2 | | 6 | 7 | 9 | 4 | | 3 |
| 3 | 7 | | | 8 | 4 | 2 | | |

B)

| | | | | | | | | |
|---|---|---|---|---|---|---|---|---|
| 3 | 8 | | 9 | | | 5 | 4 | 2 |
| | 4 | 1 | | 5 | 2 | | 3 | 6 |
| 2 | | | | 8 | | | 9 | 7 |
| 4 | 9 | | | 1 | 6 | 7 | 5 | 3 |
| 7 | | | | | | 6 | | 1 |
| 6 | | 2 | | | | 4 | 8 | |
| 1 | | 9 | 8 | 2 | 5 | 3 | | 4 |
| | 3 | 4 | 6 | 7 | 9 | | | 8 |
| 8 | 2 | 6 | 1 | 4 | | 9 | 7 | |

## C)

| | | | | | | | | |
|---|---|---|---|---|---|---|---|---|
| 5 | 9 | 7 | 4 | 3 | | | | |
| | 2 | 1 | 5 | 7 | | 3 | 4 | 9 |
| 3 | | 8 | 9 | | | 7 | 5 | |
| 8 | 3 | | 7 | | 1 | | | 4 |
| 2 | 1 | | 8 | | | 6 | 3 | 7 |
| 4 | 7 | | 2 | | 3 | 8 | 1 | 5 |
| | | 4 | 1 | 8 | | 2 | | 3 |
| 7 | | 3 | | 2 | | 5 | | 1 |
| | 6 | | 3 | 9 | | | 7 | 8 |

## D)

| | | | | | | | | |
|---|---|---|---|---|---|---|---|---|
| 2 | | | | 4 | 6 | 8 | | 1 |
| | 4 | 3 | 2 | | 1 | 6 | 5 | |
| | 8 | 6 | | 3 | 7 | 2 | 9 | 4 |
| | | 9 | | 2 | 8 | 3 | 4 | |
| 6 | | | 3 | | | 9 | 7 | 8 |
| 8 | 3 | | 6 | 7 | 9 | | 2 | |
| 4 | | 5 | | 1 | 3 | | | 2 |
| 3 | 2 | 1 | | 6 | 5 | | | |
| | 6 | 8 | 4 | 9 | 2 | 5 | | |

## E)

| | | | | | | | | |
|---|---|---|---|---|---|---|---|---|
| 5 | 9 | | | 3 | 1 | | | 2 |
| 2 | 4 | 8 | | | | | 7 | 3 |
| 6 | | 3 | | | 4 | 5 | 9 | 8 |
| 1 | 6 | 5 | | 4 | 3 | 8 | | 9 |
| 8 | | 4 | 1 | | | 3 | | |
| 7 | 3 | 9 | 5 | 2 | 8 | 4 | 1 | |
| 3 | | | | 9 | 7 | 2 | 6 | |
| | 7 | 2 | | 8 | 5 | 9 | 3 | 1 |
| | | 6 | 3 | | | | 8 | |

## F)

| | | | | | | | | |
|---|---|---|---|---|---|---|---|---|
| 7 | 4 | | 6 | 2 | | 3 | 8 | 9 |
| | | 2 | 7 | | | | 6 | 4 |
| 1 | | 3 | 4 | 9 | 8 | | 7 | 2 |
| | | | 1 | | 9 | 2 | 4 | 3 |
| 4 | 3 | 1 | | 6 | 2 | | | |
| 2 | | 9 | 3 | 4 | 5 | 6 | | 8 |
| 9 | 1 | 4 | 5 | | | 8 | 2 | 6 |
| 5 | 8 | 6 | | 1 | | | 3 | |
| 3 | 2 | | 9 | | | | | |

# 31. Jigsaw Crossword

The aim of this game is to place the filled in crossword pieces into the grid to make a complete crossword. Try and use the pieces to get you started. Each word has two pieces to form the full word, and each puzzle will have a theme.

A)

This one is all about colours...

| | | | |
|---|---|---|---|
| R | PI | LOW | NK |
| YEL | EN | ITE | VIO |
| UE | IGO | BLA | NGE |
| GRE | LET | WH | CK |
| ED | IND | ORA | BL |

B)

... while this one is fruit and veg

| | | | |
|---|---|---|---|
| APP | LEM | KIN | PE |
| ANA | PUMP | ATO | VE |
| BROC | BAN | COLI | ON |
| WI | KI | BERRY | GRA |
| LE | OLI | STRAW | TOM |

# 32. Sudoku XV

**Can you work your way through these Japanese puzzles, featuring Roman numerals?**

## The Rules:

- You must place the numbers 1-9 into the grids without repeating any number in a row, column, or marked box.
- The difference comes from the 'X' and 'V' marked between some squares. This signifies that those two numbers must add up to 5 for 'V', and 10 for 'X'.

Try your best to solve these puzzles.

A)

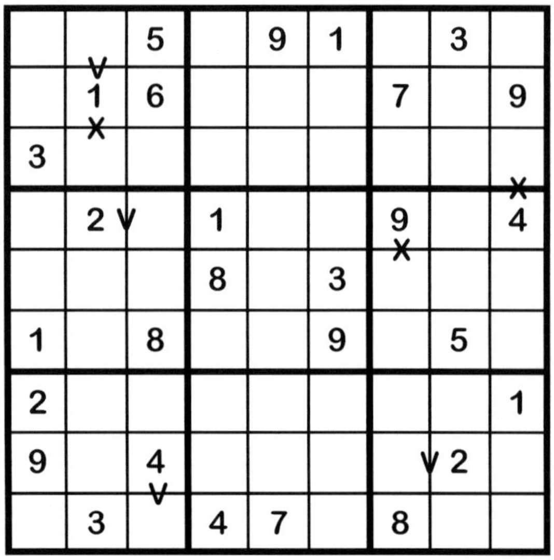

B)

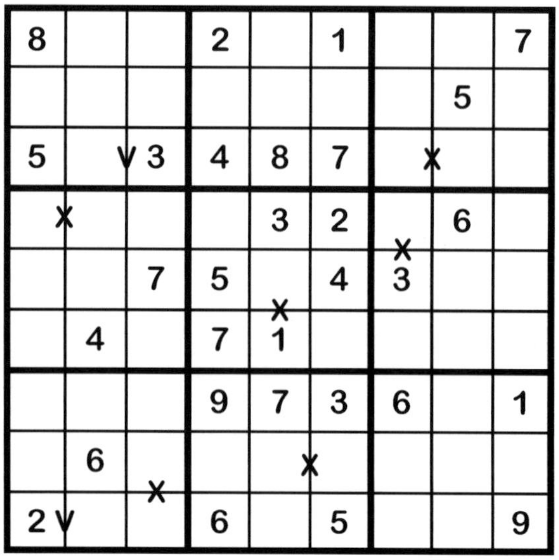

## C)

| | | | | | | | | |
|---|---|---|---|---|---|---|---|---|
| 5 | | | 2 | | | 9 | | |
| | | 9 | | 4 | 6 | | 8 | |
| 3 | | | | | 7 | 5 | 1 | |
| | 5 | | | 6 | | | 4 | |
| | | | 3 | 5 | 4 | | | |
| | 6 | | | 9 | | | 3 | |
| | | 1 | 8 | | | | | 7 |
| | 7 | | 6 | 1 | | 2 | | |
| | | 5 | | | 9 | | | 3 |

## D)

| | | | | | | | | |
|---|---|---|---|---|---|---|---|---|
| 3 | | 4 | | | 2 | | 6 | |
| | 6 | 1 | | | 9 | | | 4 |
| | | | | | 6 | | 5 | |
| | | 2 | | | 1 | | | 7 |
| | | 7 | | 6 | | | | |
| 5 | | | 9 | | | 1 | | |
| | 1 | | 3 | | | 7 | | |
| 2 | | | 6 | | | 5 | 4 | |
| | 8 | | 2 | | | 6 | | 3 |

## E)

| | | | | | | | | |
|---|---|---|---|---|---|---|---|---|
| 8 | 5 | | 7 | | | 2 | | |
| 7 | | | 2 | 8 | | 3 | | |
| | | 1 | | | 4 | 8 | | |
| | | | | | | | 1 | 7 |
| 4 | | | 1 | 5 | 2 | | | 8 |
| 3 | 1 | | | | | | | |
| | | 4 | 3 | | | 7 | | |
| | | 6 | | 2 | | | | 3 |
| | | 8 | | | 6 | | 5 | 2 |

## F)

| | | | | | | | | |
|---|---|---|---|---|---|---|---|---|
| 4 | 5 | | | 2 | 7 | 9 | | 8 |
| | | | | 3 | | | 1 | |
| | | 2 | | | 8 | | 5 | |
| | | | 2 | 8 | | 4 | | 3 |
| | | | | | | | | |
| 7 | | 9 | | 1 | 6 | | | |
| | | | 7 | | | 3 | | |
| | 4 | | | 6 | | | | |
| 2 | | 3 | 8 | 9 | | | | 6 |

# 33. Quiz

Can you guess the answer of these challenging general knowledge questions?

A) Which continent are tigers found on in the wild?

B) What is a group of elephants called?

C) Which big cat is the fastest?

D) What is the largest animal on Earth?

E) Which continent would you find Nepal on?

F) Which country has the highest population?

G) What is the large desert in North Africa called?

H) How many oceans are there?

I) What city does the Pope live in?

J) Which country would you find the Taj Mahal in?

K) What is the name of the largest coral reef, found near Australia?

L) Which planet in our solar system is the largest?

M) What would you be drinking if you drank H2O?

N) What sort of animal can be called a feline?

O) Which animals use wood to build dams?

P) Which planet would you find Olympus Mons on, the largest mountain in our solar system?

# 34. Tatamibari

Can you separate these symbols into their own rooms, and solve these puzzles?

**The Rules:**

- Each room must contain a symbol, and be the correct shape according to the symbol. Each line shows that the room is long in the same direction (a — means that the line is longer across)
- Every cell in the grid must be used within the rooms
- Rooms cannot be part of a four way junction, where the corners line up into a cross

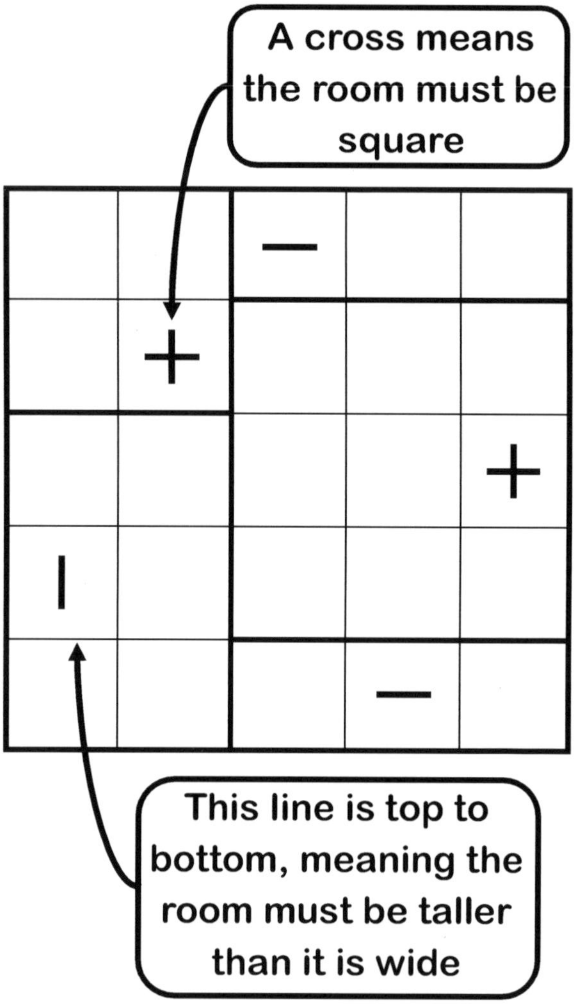


Try your best to solve these puzzles.

A)

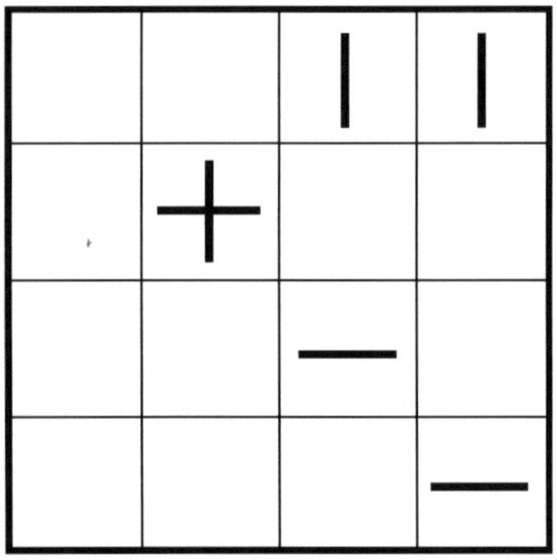

B)

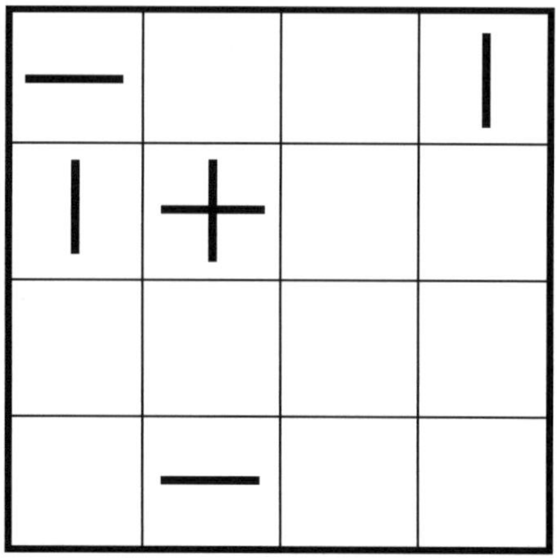

C)

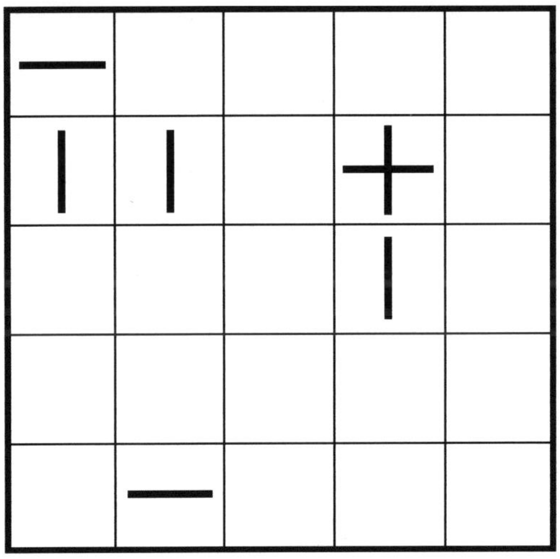

D)

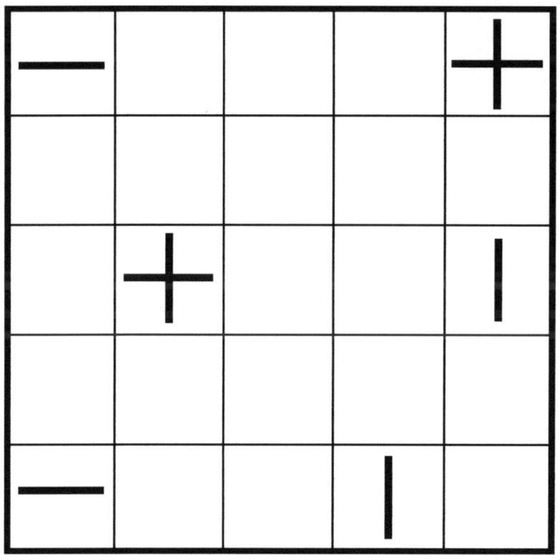

Try solving the squares first, and use that to guide how the line shapes fit together

E)

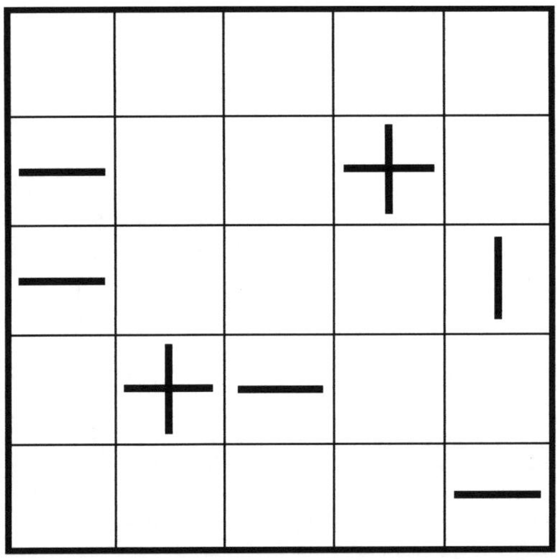

F)

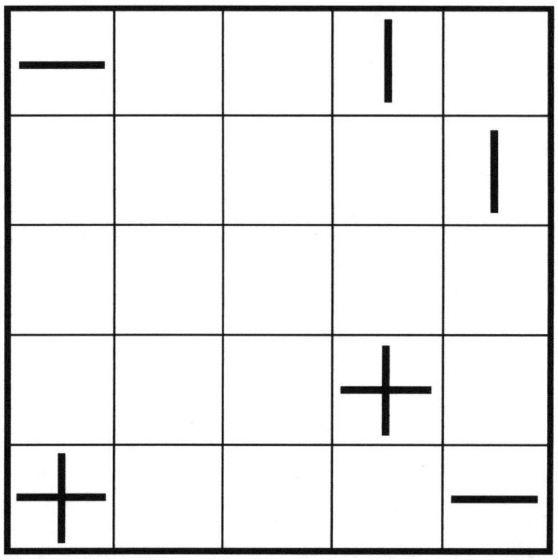

# 35. Four Step

Can you find the right path through these puzzles?

**The Rules:**

- By drawing a line, you must connect the first 1 to the last 4 by following a 1-2-3-4 pattern throughout the grid, using all the numbers
- The starting '1' and ending '4' are marked in the circled squares, and each square can only be used once.
- The line can go in any direction, including diagonally, but may not cross itself.

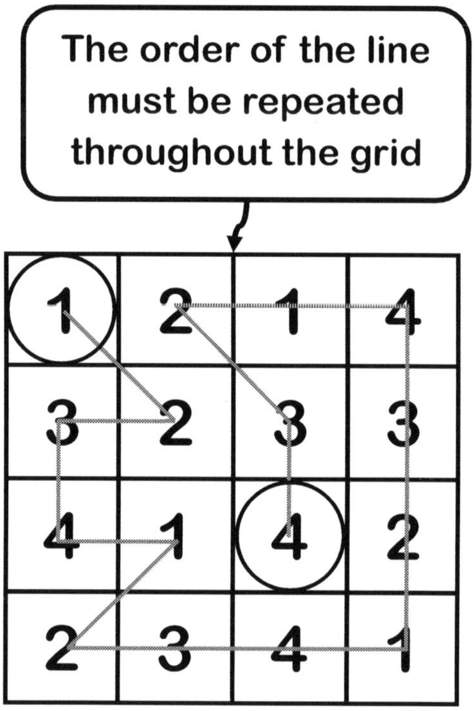


Try your best to solve these puzzles.

A)

| | | | |
|---|---|---|---|
| 4 | 1 | 2 | 3 |
| 3 | 2 | 1 | 4 |
| 2 | 3 | 4 | 1 |
| (1) | (4) | 3 | 2 |

B)

| | | | |
|---|---|---|---|
| 1 | 2 | 3 | 4 |
| 4 | 3 | 2 | 1 |
| 2 | (4) | 3 | 2 |
| 1 | 4 | 3 | (1) |

C)

| | | | |
|---|---|---|---|
| 1 | 2 | 2 | 3 |
| 4 | 3 | 1 | 4 |
| 1 | 4 | 2 | 1 |
| 2 | 3 | 3 | 4 |

D)

| | | | |
|---|---|---|---|
| 1 | 2 | 3 | 4 |
| 3 | 4 | 4 | 3 |
| 2 | 2 | 1 | 2 |
| 1 | 3 | 4 | 1 |

E)

| | | | | | |
|---|---|---|---|---|---|
| 3 | 4 | 1 | 2 | 3 | 4 |
| 1 | 2 | 2 | 1 | 4 | 1 |
| 4 | 1 | 4 | 3 | 3 | 2 |
| 3 | 2 | 1 | 4 | 3 | 2 |
| 2 | 3 | 2 | 3 | 4 | 1 |
| 1 | 4 | 1 | 2 | 3 | 4 |

F)

| | | | | | |
|---|---|---|---|---|---|
| 2 | 3 | 4 | 1 | 2 | 3 |
| 1 | 3 | 2 | 3 | 2 | 4 |
| 4 | 4 | 1 | 4 | 1 | 1 |
| 3 | 1 | 4 | 4 | 3 | 2 |
| 2 | 2 | 3 | 2 | 1 | 4 |
| 1 | 4 | 3 | 1 | 2 | 3 |

# 36. Circle Words

**Can you spell out the answers to these questions by using the letters in the circle? Each letter can only be used once.**

**Cross through each letter after you have used it to help you keep track**

**A)**

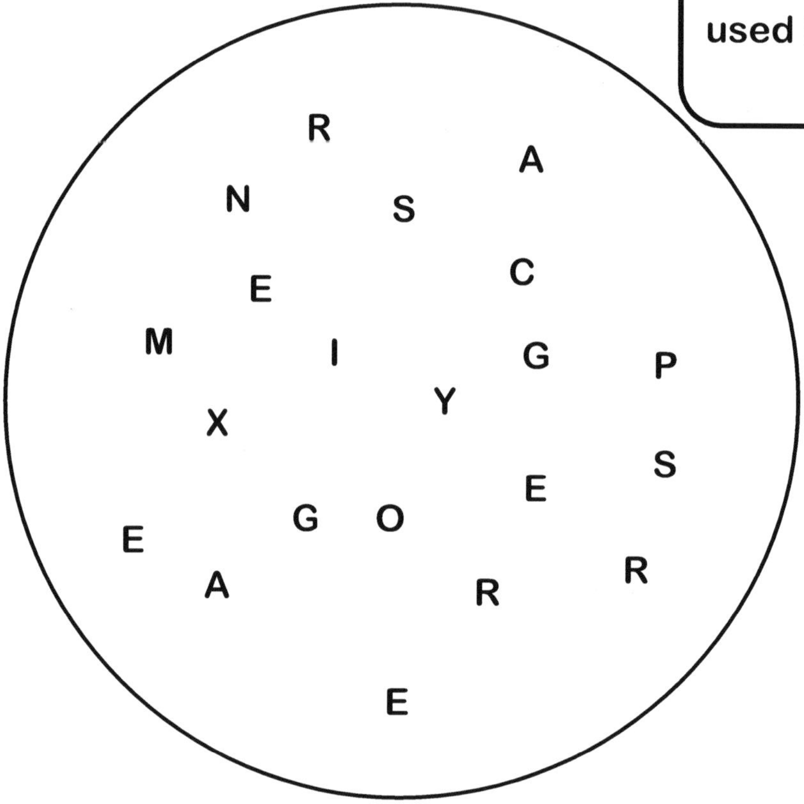


**In which country were the Olympics first held?**

..........................................................................................................

**What is the capital of France?**

..........................................................................................................

**What element do we need to breathe in to survive?**

..........................................................................................................

**What planet is also known as the Red Planet?**

..........................................................................................................

B)

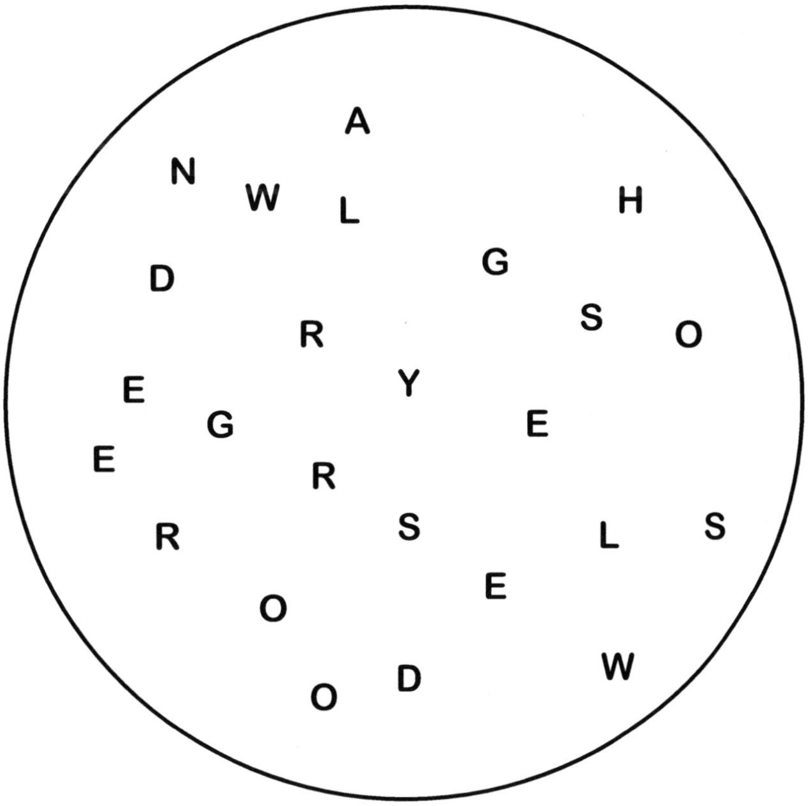


Which Scandinavian country begins with S?

..........................................................................................................

What animal shares its name with a type of chestnut, also called conkers?

..........................................................................................................

What does the first W stand for in the internet term WWW?

..........................................................................................................

What are the stone creatures who are found on

# 37. How Big?

Take a guess and see how close you can get with these impossible questions. Rather than trying to guess the correct answer, see if you can guess closer than your family and friends.

A) How many bridges does Hamburg, The City of Bridges, in Germany have?

1) Over 1200    2) Over 1800    3) Over 2300

B) How many pieces did the largest ever jigsaw have?

1) 325,678    2) 551,232    3) 834,945

C) What is the most press ups ever done in a day?

1) 25,654    2) 32,596    3) 46,001

D) How long did the oldest ever person live?

1) 115 years, 245 days 2) 122 years, 164 days
3) 127 years, 98 days

E) How big would a cube of one million grains of sand be?

1) One cubic centimetre 2) One cubic inch
3) One cubic foot

F) How many cups of coffee are drank in America every single day?

1) 200 million 2) 300 million 3) 400 million

G) Surprisingly, the biggest tyre manufacturer in the world is Lego, but how many tyres do they make per year?

1) 700 million 2) 850 million 3) 1 Billion

# 38. In Proportion

Can you draw these shapes to the correct sizes?

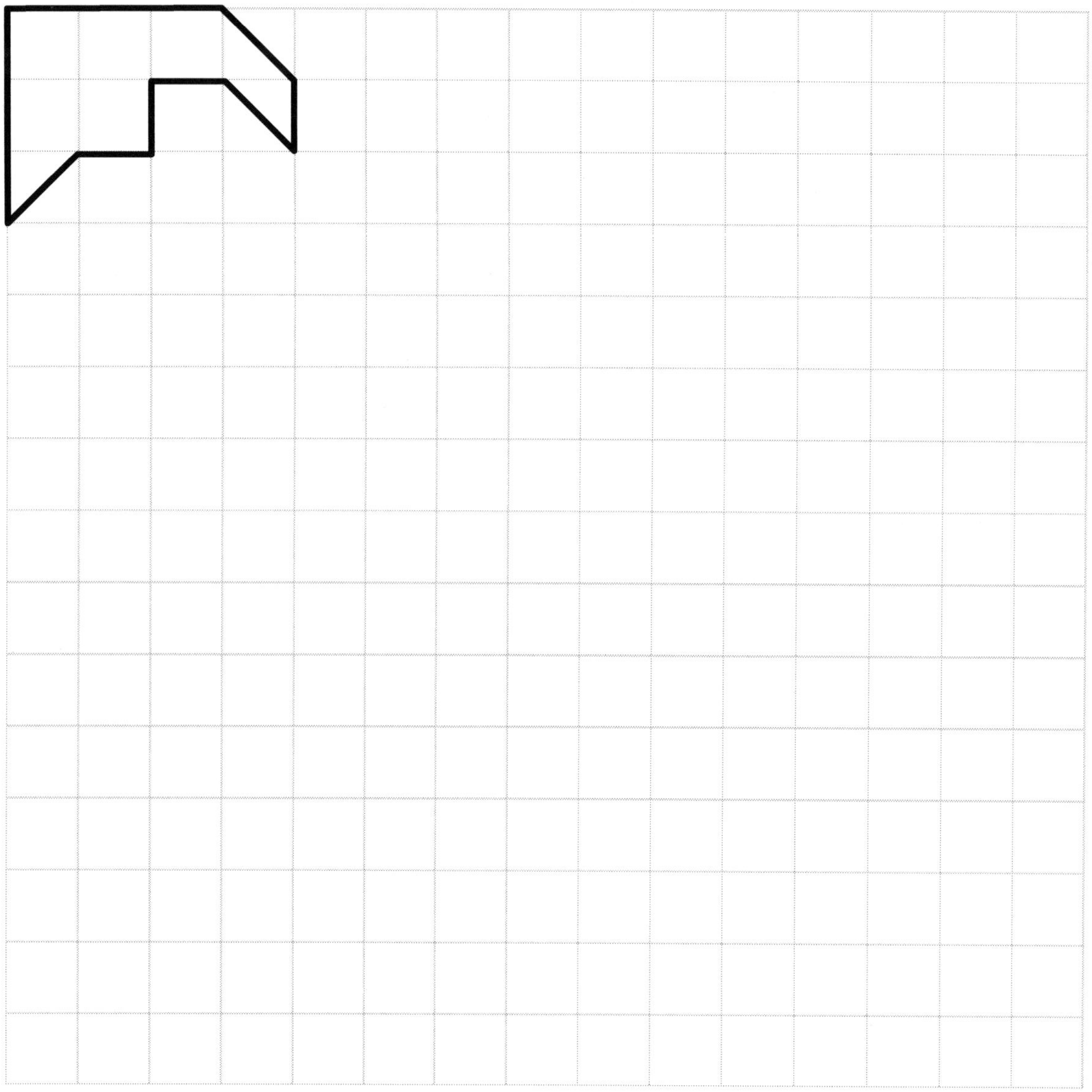

Can you draw this shape again, but three times as big?

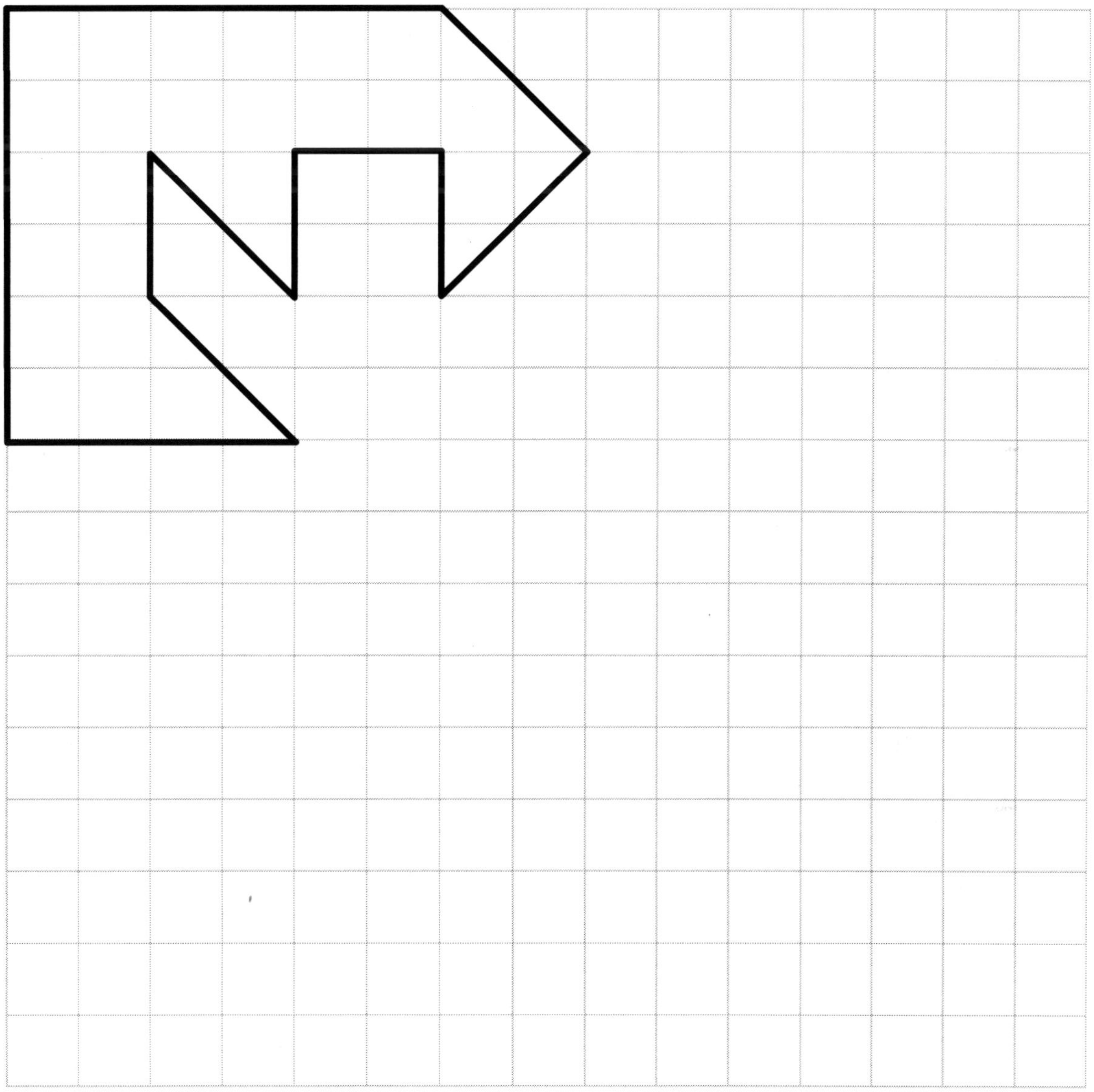

**Can you draw this shape again, but half the size?**

# 39. Anagrams

Can you unscramble each of these words to find out the real word?

CHRISTMAS

A) KTUEYR

B) PERNTSS

C) ILDYAHO

D) ETER

E) ANSTA

F) DPDUGNI

G) BUBAEL

H) LNAGE

I) DORUHPL

J) NSWO

K) RKCACRE

L) EENDIERR

## ZOO ANIMALS

M) LONI

N) RTGIE

O) GFIRFAE

P) YMENOK

Q) TELPANHE

R) OHRIN

S) KTEMREA

T) ECETHAH

U) REBA

V) WLFO

## CHILDREN'S NAMES

W) AJMSE

X) XAEL

Y) MAAD

Z) VDIDA

AB) GGEEOR

AC) CLOTETHAR

AD) LACIE

AE) EKAT

# 40. Keisuke

Can you place these numbers in the correct positions, and fill in these challenging Japanese puzzles?

## The Rules:

- Each clue given will either be written left to right, or downwards within the grid
- Just like a crossword, each clue must overlap correctly

Try your best to solve these puzzles.

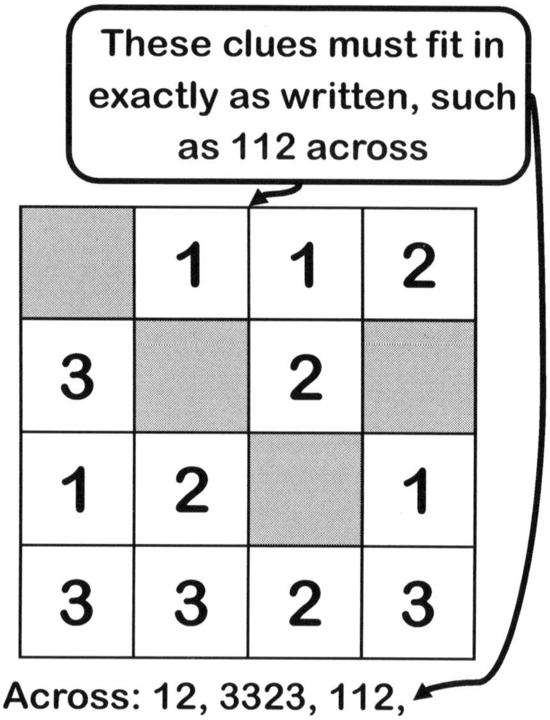


Across: 12, 3323, 112,

Down: 313, 13, 23, 12

A)

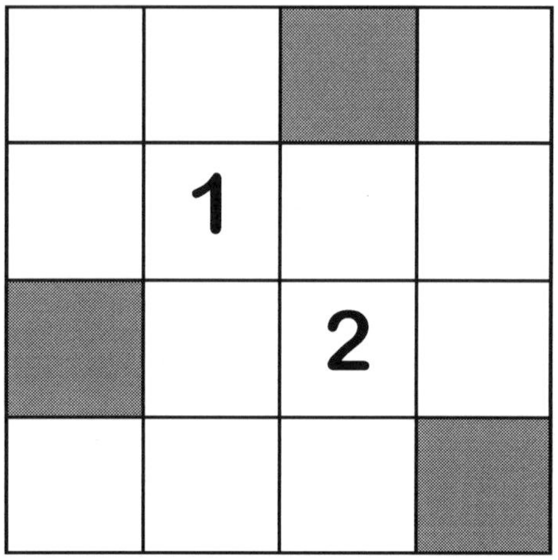


Across: 2113, 223, 23, 231

Down: 22, 3123, 121, 133

B)

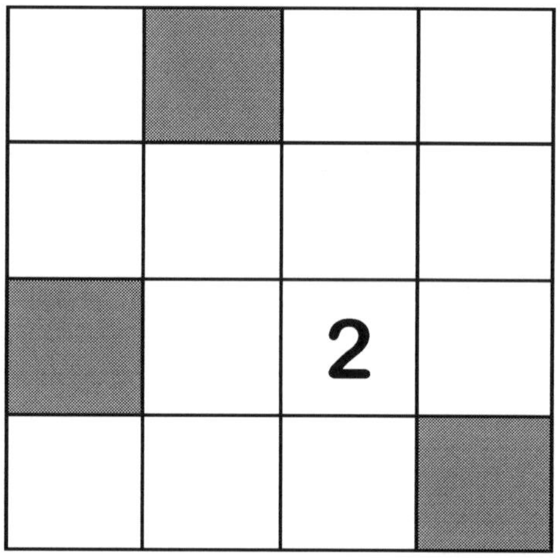


Across: 123, 1313, 23, 113

Down: 21, 333, 2123, 311

C)

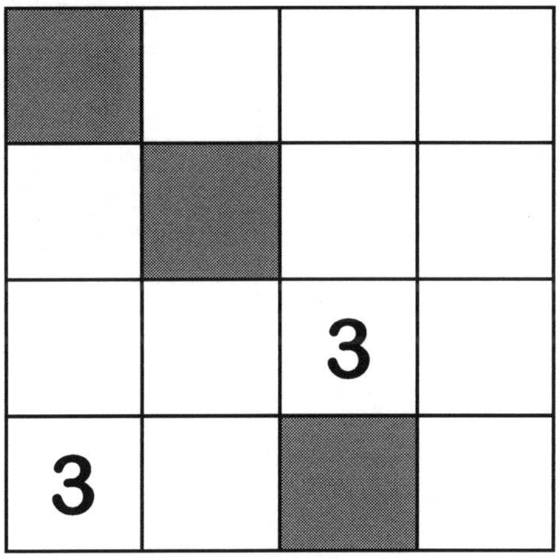


Across: 2233, 112, 31, 32

Down: 323, 133, 22, 2132

D)

Across: 21, 213, 111, 32

Down: 11, 23, 213, 331

E)

Across: 13, 31, 22, 2133, 111, 23131

Down: 22, 33, 1311, 11, 312, 13, 131

F)

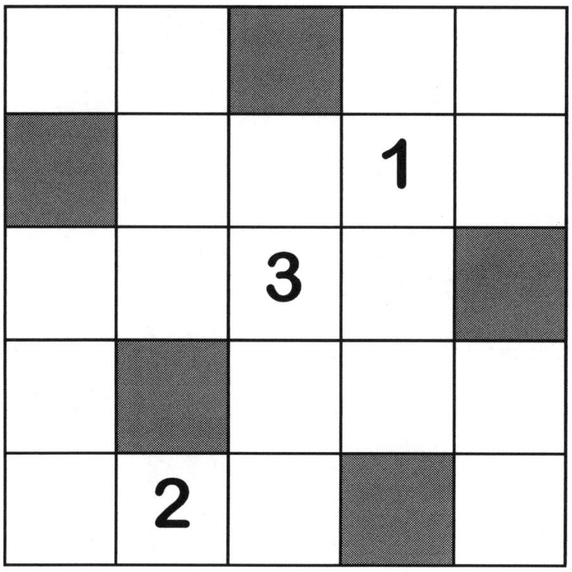


Across: 11, 2312, 3133, 23, 322, 321

Down: 3332, 2132, 32, 11, 121, 333

1A)

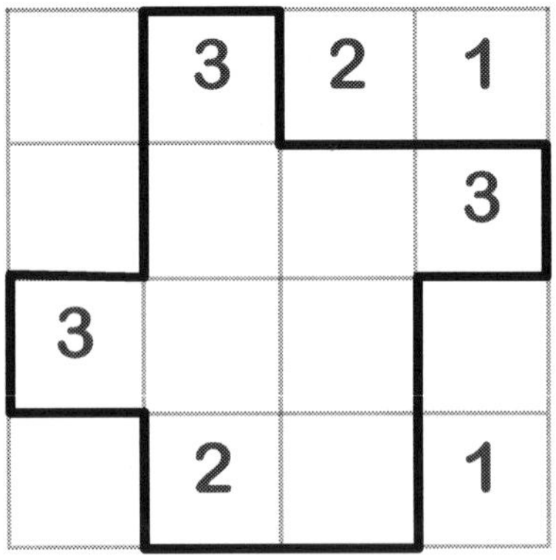


1B)

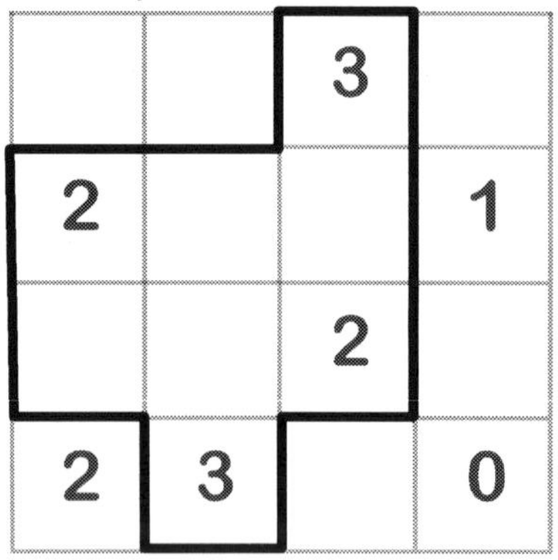


1C)

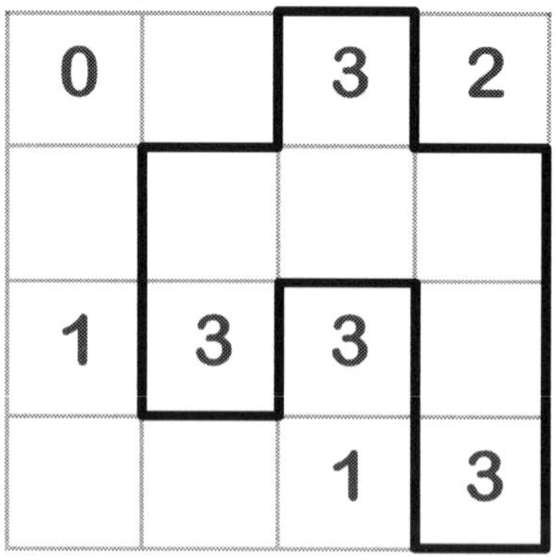


1D)

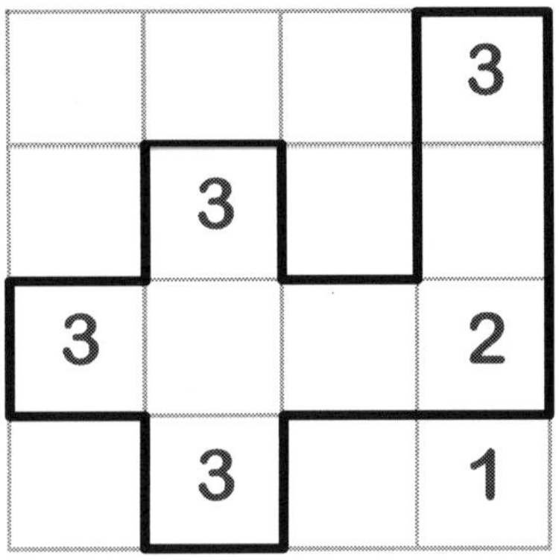


1E)

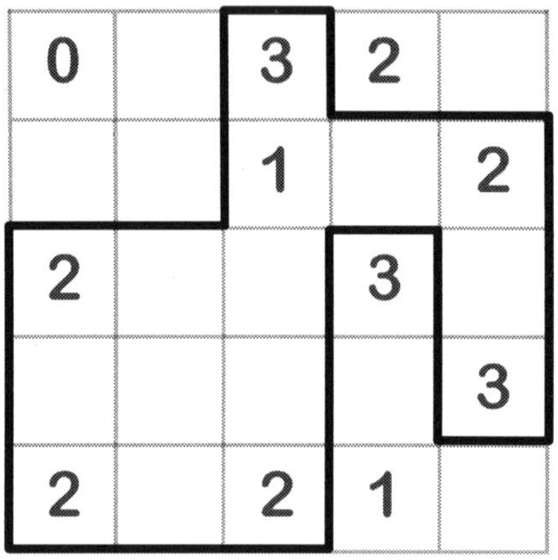


1F)

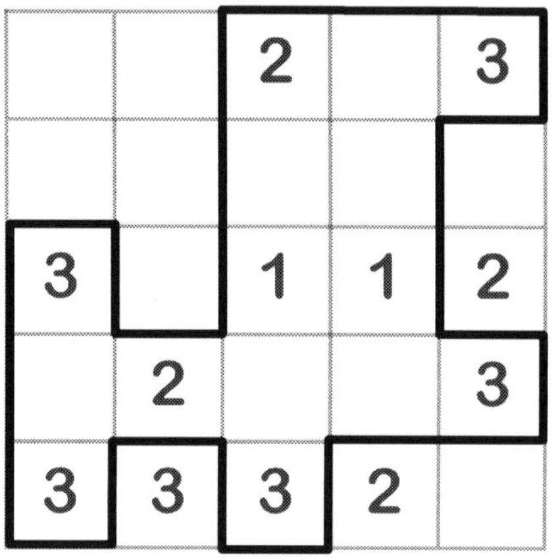


2A)

BAG
BAR
FAR
FOR

2B)

SAD
SAY
HAY
HEY

2C)

LEG
LAG
LAP
MAP

2D)

PAY
RAY
RAD
RED

2E)

BUSH
BASH
CASH
CASE
CAKE

2F)

MICE
LICE
LIME
LIMP
LAMP

3A)

| | | | | | |
|---|---|---|---|---|---|
| 4 | 2 | 3 | 5 | 1 | 6 |
| 5 | 6 | 1 | 3 | 2 | 4 |
| 1 | 5 | 4 | 2 | 6 | 3 |
| 2 | 3 | 6 | 4 | 5 | 1 |
| 3 | 1 | 2 | 6 | 4 | 5 |
| 6 | 4 | 5 | 1 | 3 | 2 |

3B)

| | | | | | |
|---|---|---|---|---|---|
| 6 | 4 | 3 | 2 | 5 | 1 |
| 2 | 5 | 1 | 3 | 6 | 4 |
| 3 | 6 | 4 | 5 | 1 | 2 |
| 5 | 1 | 2 | 4 | 3 | 6 |
| 1 | 2 | 5 | 6 | 4 | 3 |
| 4 | 3 | 6 | 1 | 2 | 5 |

3C)

| | | | | | | | | |
|---|---|---|---|---|---|---|---|---|
| 8 | 4 | 7 | 6 | 5 | 9 | 2 | 1 | 3 |
| 9 | 3 | 1 | 2 | 7 | 4 | 6 | 8 | 5 |
| 2 | 5 | 6 | 1 | 3 | 8 | 4 | 7 | 9 |
| 6 | 2 | 8 | 4 | 9 | 7 | 3 | 5 | 1 |
| 4 | 7 | 9 | 5 | 1 | 3 | 8 | 6 | 2 |
| 5 | 1 | 3 | 8 | 2 | 6 | 9 | 4 | 7 |
| 7 | 8 | 2 | 3 | 6 | 5 | 1 | 9 | 4 |
| 1 | 9 | 4 | 7 | 8 | 2 | 5 | 3 | 6 |
| 3 | 6 | 5 | 9 | 4 | 1 | 7 | 2 | 8 |

3D)

| | | | | | | | | |
|---|---|---|---|---|---|---|---|---|
| 3 | 9 | 5 | 1 | 6 | 4 | 7 | 8 | 2 |
| 2 | 6 | 7 | 8 | 9 | 5 | 1 | 3 | 4 |
| 1 | 8 | 4 | 7 | 2 | 3 | 5 | 9 | 6 |
| 5 | 4 | 2 | 3 | 8 | 9 | 6 | 1 | 7 |
| 9 | 1 | 3 | 6 | 7 | 2 | 8 | 4 | 5 |
| 6 | 7 | 8 | 5 | 4 | 1 | 3 | 2 | 9 |
| 4 | 3 | 6 | 9 | 5 | 8 | 2 | 7 | 1 |
| 8 | 5 | 9 | 2 | 1 | 7 | 4 | 6 | 3 |
| 7 | 2 | 1 | 4 | 3 | 6 | 9 | 5 | 8 |

3E)

| | | | | | | | | |
|---|---|---|---|---|---|---|---|---|
| 3 | 2 | 1 | 5 | 8 | 9 | 4 | 7 | 6 |
| 4 | 7 | 8 | 3 | 2 | 6 | 5 | 9 | 1 |
| 5 | 9 | 6 | 4 | 7 | 1 | 2 | 8 | 3 |
| 2 | 8 | 5 | 6 | 1 | 7 | 9 | 3 | 4 |
| 6 | 4 | 7 | 2 | 9 | 3 | 8 | 1 | 5 |
| 1 | 3 | 9 | 8 | 4 | 5 | 6 | 2 | 7 |
| 7 | 5 | 3 | 9 | 6 | 8 | 1 | 4 | 2 |
| 8 | 1 | 2 | 7 | 5 | 4 | 3 | 6 | 9 |
| [illegible] | [illegible] | [illegible] | [illegible] | [illegible] | [illegible] | [illegible] | [illegible] | [illegible] |

3F)

| | | | | | | | | |
|---|---|---|---|---|---|---|---|---|
| 8 | 3 | 9 | 1 | 7 | 4 | 2 | 6 | 5 |
| 5 | 4 | 6 | 8 | 2 | 3 | 1 | 9 | 7 |
| 7 | 2 | 1 | 5 | 6 | 9 | 4 | 3 | 8 |
| 4 | 5 | 2 | 3 | 8 | 7 | 6 | 1 | 9 |
| 6 | 8 | 3 | 9 | 1 | 5 | 7 | 2 | 4 |
| 9 | 1 | 7 | 2 | 4 | 6 | 5 | 8 | 3 |
| 2 | 7 | 4 | 6 | 9 | 8 | 3 | 5 | 1 |
| 3 | 6 | 8 | 4 | 5 | 1 | 9 | 7 | 2 |
| [illegible] | [illegible] | [illegible] | [illegible] | [illegible] | [illegible] | [illegible] | [illegible] | [illegible] |

4A) DAD, DOG, DOT, LAD, LAG, LED, LEG, LET, LOG, LOT, PAD, PAT, PEG, PET, POD, POT, SAD, SAG, SAT, SET, SOD, SOG

4B) FAN, FAT, FIN, FIT, FUN, HAM, HAT, HIM, HIT, HUM, HUT, RAM, RAN, RAT, RIM, RUM, RUN, RUT, SAT, SIN, SIM, SIT, SUN, SUM

4C) BACK, BALL, BALM, BEAM, BEAK, BECK, BELL, PACK, PALL, PALM, PEAK, PEAL, PECK, PEEL PRAM, SACK, SEAM, SHAM, TACK, TALK, TEAK, TELL, TRAM

5A) The square is the heaviest while the circle is the lightest. Five triangles are needed to balance the scales

5B) The triangle is the heaviest while the square is the lightest. Seven circles are needed to balance the scales.

A square weighs 2 A circle weighs 3 A triangle weighs 5

6A): AI: SAID, GAIN, CLAIM, PAINT, PRAISE, FAIRLY

6B): OA: GOAL, TOAD, BOARD, GLOAT, THROAT, COARSE

6C): ETH: TEETH, ETHIC, METHOD, LETHAL, WHETHER, RETHINK

6D): LAT: LATER, SPLAT, PLATES, FLATLY, ISOLATE, RELATED

6E): OR: BORN, SHORT, BEFORE TH: BATH, THING, RHYTHM

7A)

| | | |
|---|---|---|
| 9 | 2 | 4 |
| 5 | 7 | 3 |
| 1 | 6 | 8 |

7B)

| | | |
|---|---|---|
| 2 | 9 | 7 |
| 10 | 5 | 3 |
| 6 | 4 | 8 |

7C)

| | | |
|---|---|---|
| 6 | 8 | 10 |
| 7 | 12 | 5 |
| 11 | 4 | 9 |

7D)

| | | |
|---|---|---|
| 10 | 3 | 8 |
| 5 | 7 | 9 |
| 6 | 11 | 4 |

7E)

| | | | |
|---|---|---|---|
| 8 | 11 | 14 | 1 |
| 13 | 2 | 7 | 12 |
| 3 | 16 | 9 | 6 |
| 10 | 5 | 4 | 15 |

7F)

| | | | |
|---|---|---|---|
| 17 | 4 | 3 | 14 |
| 6 | 11 | 12 | 9 |
| 10 | 7 | 8 | 13 |
| 5 | 16 | 15 | 2 |

8A) ENGLAND, GERMANY, FRANCE, SPAIN, PORTUGAL

8B) SHEEP, GOAT, HORSE, COW, CHICKEN

8C) TRUMPET, SAXOPHONE, VIOLIN, CLARINET, HARP

8D) TENNIS, FOOTBALL, BASKETBALL, BADMINTON, NETBALL

9A)

| | | | |
|---|---|---|---|
| | ↓8 | ↓17 | |
| 7→ | 2 | 5 | ↓3 |
| 10→ | 6 | 3 | 1 |
| | 11→ | 9 | 2 |

9B)

| | | | |
|---|---|---|---|
| | ↓11 | ↓10 | |
| 6→ | 2 | 4 | 11→ |
| 10→ | 3 | 5 | 2 |
| 16→ | 6 | 1 | 9 |

## 9C)

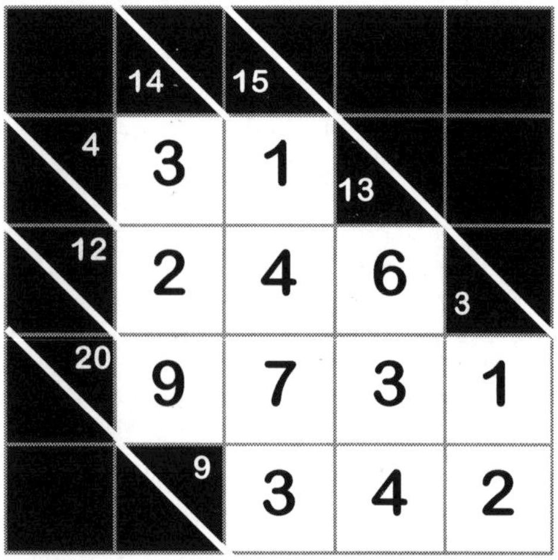


## 9D)

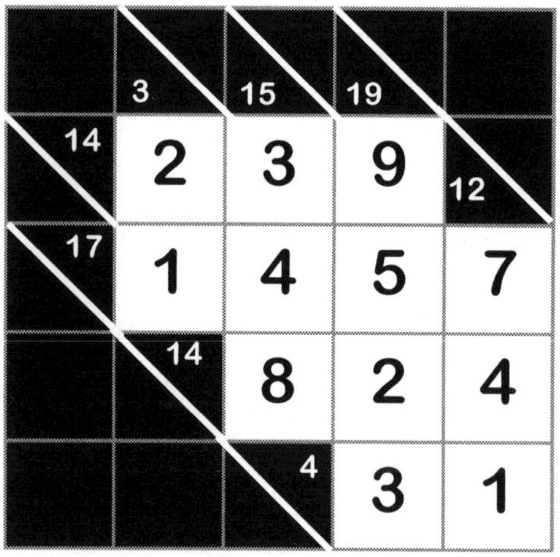


## 9E)

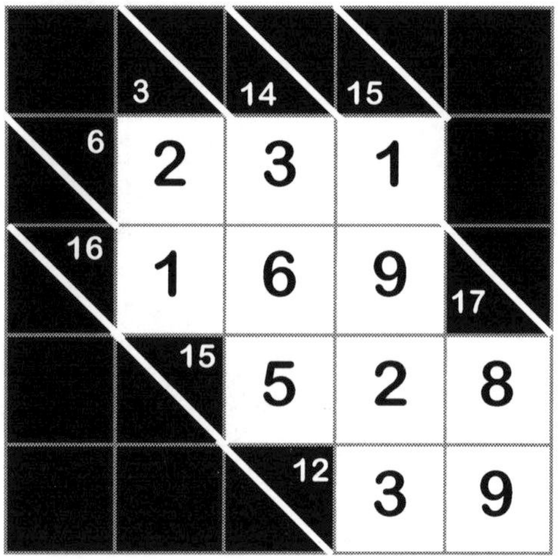


## 9F)

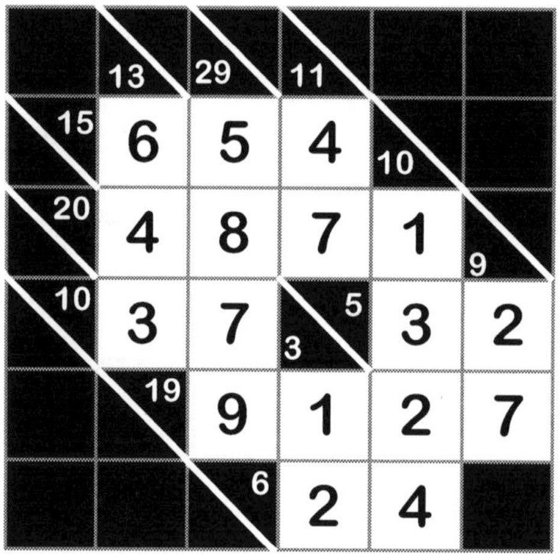


## 10A)

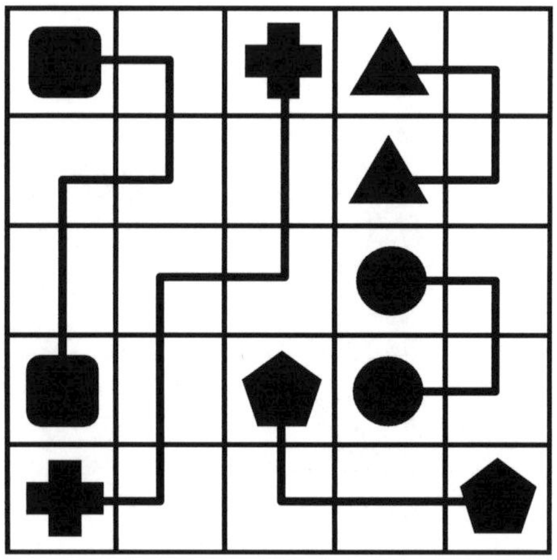

## 10B)

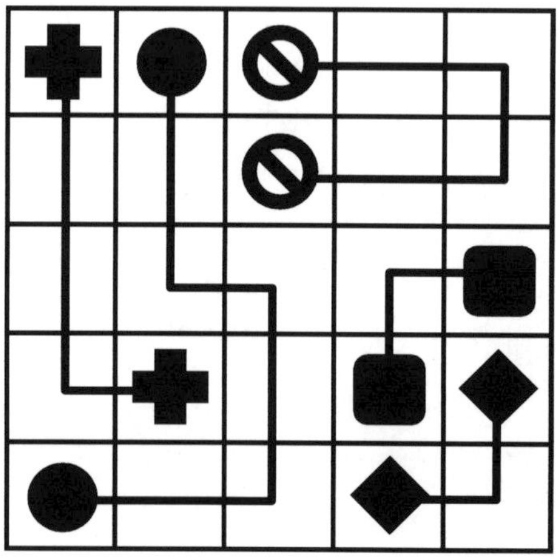

10C)

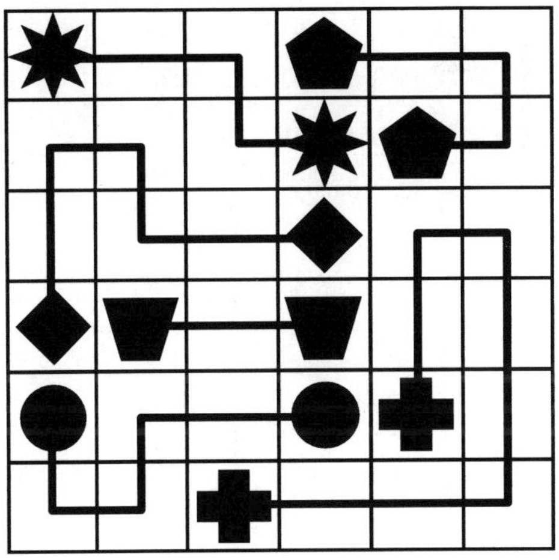

10D)

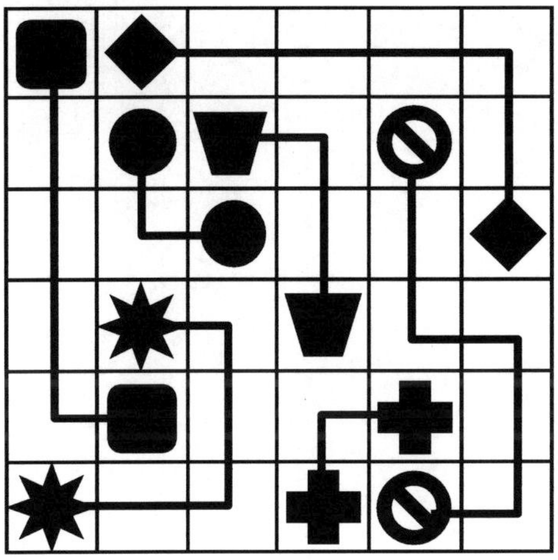

10E)

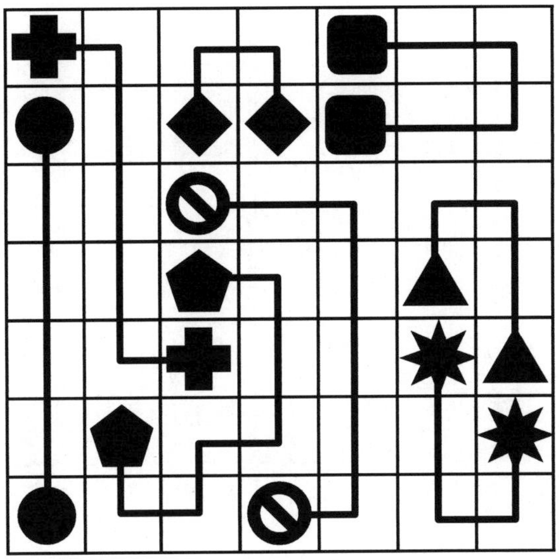

10F)

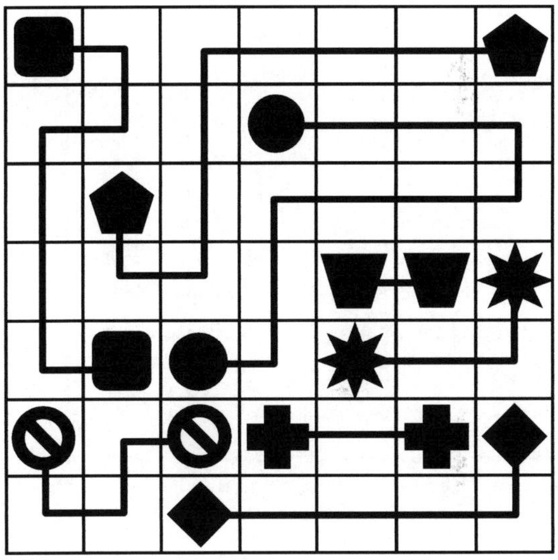

11A)

| | | | |
|---|---|---|---|
| 1 | $^{7}$3 | $^{6}$4 | 2 |
| $^{6}$2 | 4 | $^{4}$1 | 3 |
| 4 | $^{3}$2 | 3 | 1 |
| 3 | 1 | $^{6}$2 | 4 |

11B)

| | | | |
|---|---|---|---|
| $^{3}$2 | 1 | $^{5}$4 | 3 |
| $^{7}$4 | 3 | 1 | $^{3}$2 |
| $^{4}$3 | $^{6}$4 | 2 | 1 |
| 1 | 2 | $^{7}$3 | 4 |

## 11C)

| | | | |
|---|---|---|---|
| [4] 1 | 3 | [6] 2 | 4 |
| [6] 4 | 2 | [4] 3 | 1 |
| 2 | [5] 1 | 4 | 3 |
| [7] 3 | 4 | [3] 1 | 2 |

## 11D)

| | | | |
|---|---|---|---|
| 4 | [3] 1 | 2 | [7] 3 |
| [4] 3 | 2 | [5] 1 | 4 |
| 1 | 3 | 4 | 2 |
| [6] 2 | 4 | [4] 3 | 1 |

## 11E)

| | | | |
|---|---|---|---|
| [7] 3 | 4 | [3] 2 | 1 |
| [6] 2 | 1 | [7] 4 | 3 |
| 4 | [4] 3 | 1 | 2 |
| [3] 1 | 2 | [7] 3 | 4 |

## 11F)

| | | | |
|---|---|---|---|
| 3 | [3] 1 | 4 | [5] 2 |
| [6] 4 | 2 | [4] 1 | 3 |
| 2 | 4 | 3 | 1 |
| [4] 1 | 3 | [6] 2 | 4 |

**12A)**
100 x 2 = 200
10 x 10 = 100
4 x 4 = 16
200 + 100 - 16 = 284

**12B)**
10 x 5 = 50
50 x 3 = 150
150 + 2 + 1 + 1 = 154

**12C)**
7 + 3 = 10
10 x 25 = 250
250 + 8 + 4 + 1 = 263

**12D)**
100 x 4 = 400
7 x 6 = 42
400 - 42 - 5 - 2 = 351

**12E)**
5 + 6 = 11
11 x 50 = 550
7 x 6 = 42
550 + 42 - 4 = 588

**12F)**
7 x 2 + 1 = 15
15 x 50 = 750
750 - 10 - 9 = 731

13A)

| | | | |
|---|---|---|---|
| 3 | | | |
| 4 | | 2 | |
| | | | |
| 3 | | | 4 |

13B)

| | | | |
|---|---|---|---|
| | | 3 | |
| | | | |
| 3 | | 4 | |
| 2 | | 4 | |

13C)

| | | | | |
|---|---|---|---|---|
| | | 4 | | |
| | | 5 | | |
| 3 | | 3 | | |
| 4 | | 6 | | |
| | | | | |

13D)

| | | | | |
|---|---|---|---|---|
| 3 | | | | |
| 4 | 4 | | 4 | |
| | | | 5 | |
| | 3 | | | |
| | | | 2 | |

13E)

| | | | | | |
|---|---|---|---|---|---|
| | | | | | |
| | 4 | 4 | | | 3 |
| | 4 | | | 4 | |
| | 4 | 6 | | | |
| | | | | | 3 |
| | | 4 | | | |

13F)

| | | | | | |
|---|---|---|---|---|---|
| 3 | | | 3 | | 6 |
| | | | | | |
| | 6 | | | | |
| 4 | | 4 | | | |
| | | | | | 4 |
| 6 | | | | | |

14A)

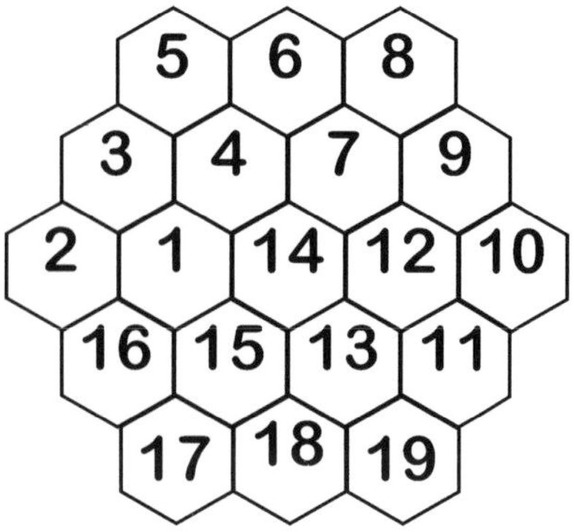


14B)

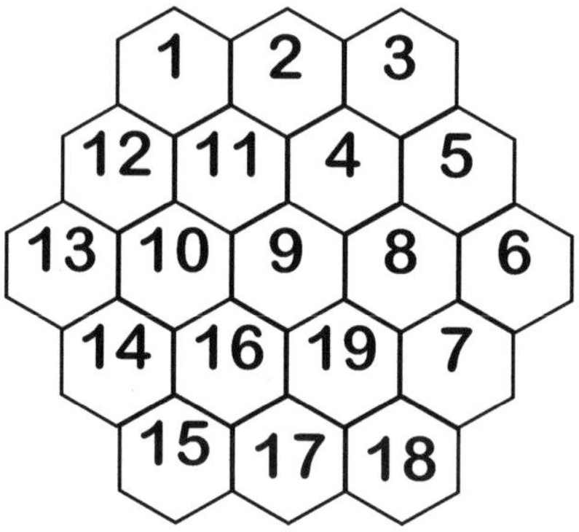


14C)

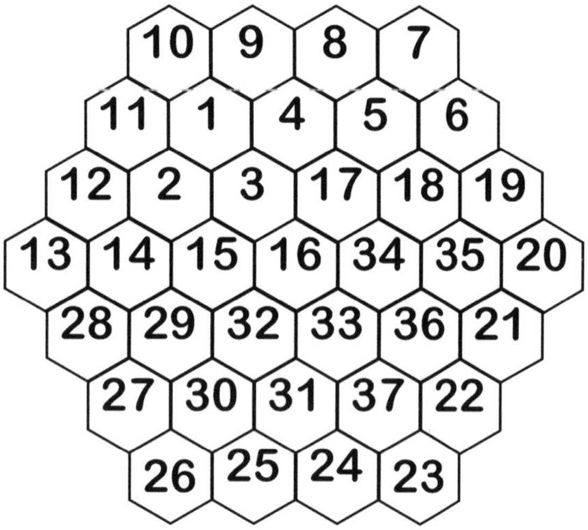


14D)

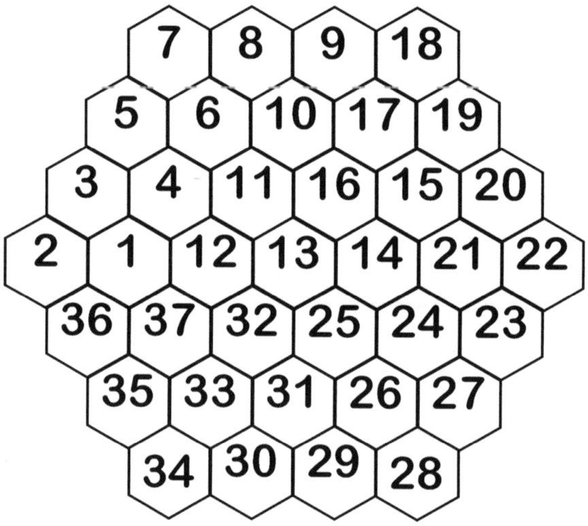


14E)

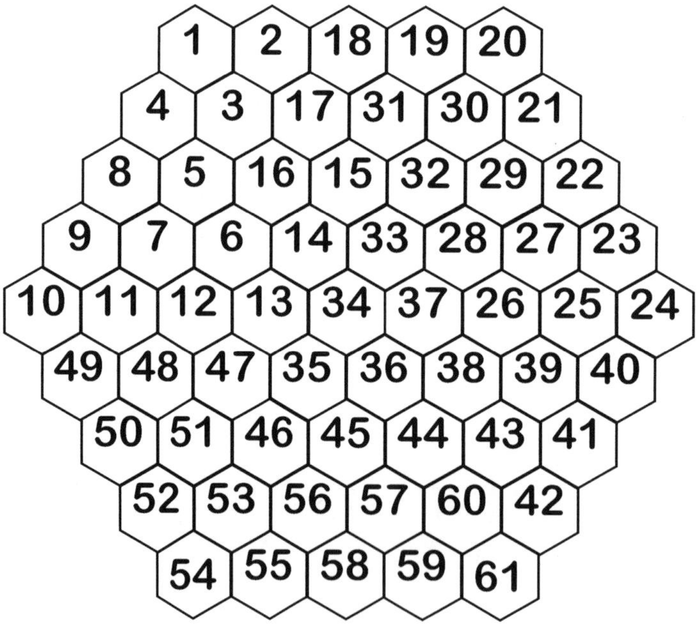

15A)

| | | | | |
|---|---|---|---|---|
| 3 | | 1 | | 8 |
| | 17 | | 20 | |
| 7 | | 6 | | 5 |
| | 24 | | 17 | |
| 9 | | 2 | | 4 |

15B)

| | | | | |
|---|---|---|---|---|
| 4 | | 7 | | 3 |
| | 28 | | 19 | |
| 9 | | 8 | | 1 |
| | 28 | | 16 | |
| 6 | | 5 | | 2 |

15C)

| | | | | |
|---|---|---|---|---|
| 2 | | 5 | | 9 |
| | 11 | | 23 | |
| 1 | | 3 | | 6 |
| | 15 | | 24 | |
| 4 | | 7 | | 8 |

15D)

| | | | | |
|---|---|---|---|---|
| 8 | | 9 | | 1 |
| | 26 | | 17 | |
| 6 | | 3 | | 4 |
| | 16 | | 19 | |
| 2 | | 5 | | 7 |

15E)

| | | | | |
|---|---|---|---|---|
| 9 | | 7 | | 4 |
| | 21 | | 18 | |
| 3 | | 2 | | 5 |
| | 14 | | 21 | |
| 1 | | 8 | | 6 |

15F)

| | | | | |
|---|---|---|---|---|
| 6 | | 8 | | 2 |
| | 22 | | 26 | |
| 1 | | 7 | | 9 |
| | 17 | | 23 | |
| 5 | | 4 | | 3 |

| | | | | | | | |
|---|---|---|---|---|---|---|---|
| 16A) | 21 | 53 | 26 | 16B) | 22 | 20 | 56 |
| 16C) | 57 | 20 | 55 | 16D) | 74 | 4 | 60 |
| 16E) | 750 | 20 | 399 | | | | |
| 17A) | 5,6 | 8,10 | 16,32 | 17B) | 15,21 | 13,16 | 21,31 |
| 17C) | 7,6 | 6,0 | 17,33 | 17D) | E,F | I,K | L,G |
| 17E) | P,F | M,H | QR,RS | | | | |

| 18A) | 18B) | 18C) |
|---|---|---|
| DESIGN | IMPACT | CINEMA |
| INSIDE | EXPAND | HONEST |
| RISING | REPAIR | NINETY |
| BESIDE | DEPART | LONELY |

19A)

| | | | | |
|---|---|---|---|---|
| 7 | + | 9 | = | 16 |
| + | | + | | + |
| 8 | + | 3 | = | 11 |
| = | | = | | = |
| 15 | + | 12 | = | 27 |

19B)

| | | | | |
|---|---|---|---|---|
| 12 | + | 14 | = | 26 |
| + | | + | | + |
| 19 | + | 4 | = | 23 |
| = | | = | | = |
| 31 | + | 18 | = | 49 |

19C)

| | | | | | | |
|---|---|---|---|---|---|---|
| 2 | + | 7 | + | 9 | = | 18 |
| + | | + | | + | | + |
| 3 | + | 4 | + | 11 | = | 18 |
| + | | + | | + | | + |
| 5 | + | 7 | + | 4 | = | 16 |
| = | | = | | = | | = |
| 10 | + | 18 | + | 24 | = | 52 |

19D)

| | | | | | | |
|---|---|---|---|---|---|---|
| 8 | + | 9 | + | 4 | = | 21 |
| + | | + | | + | | + |
| 7 | + | 6 | + | 7 | = | 20 |
| + | | + | | + | | + |
| 10 | + | 1 | + | 9 | = | 20 |
| = | | = | | = | | = |
| 25 | + | 16 | + | 20 | = | 61 |

19E)

| | | | | | | |
|---|---|---|---|---|---|---|
| 7 | + | 5 | + | 6 | = | 18 |
| + | | - | | - | | |
| 4 | + | 1 | + | 2 | = | 7 |
| - | | x | | + | | |
| 2 | x | 3 | - | 3 | = | 3 |
| = | | = | | = | | |
| 9 | | 12 | | 7 | | |

19F)

| | | | | | | |
|---|---|---|---|---|---|---|
| 8 | - | 3 | + | 12 | = | 17 |
| + | | + | | + | | |
| 11 | + | 21 | - | 17 | = | 15 |
| - | | ÷ | | - | | |
| 7 | - | 4 | + | 13 | = | 16 |
| = | | = | | = | | |
| 12 | | 6 | | 16 | | |

20A) What do you get if you cross a snowman and a vampire? Frostbite

20B) What kind of shoes do ninjas wear? Sneakers

20C) What school subject do witches like best? Spelling

21A)

| | | | | | | | | | | | | | |
|---|---|---|---|---|---|---|---|---|---|---|---|---|---|
| | | | | | | C | H | E | S | S | | | |
| | | | | | A | | | | I | | | | |
| B | R | I | D | G | E | | | | L | | | | |
| | | | | | R | | | | V | | | | |
| | | | | | O | | | | E | A | G | L | E |
| | | C | O | M | P | U | T | E | R | | | | |
| A | | | | | L | | | | | | | | |
| C | A | M | E | R | A | | | | | | | | |
| T | | | | | N | | | | | | | | |
| O | | | S | H | E | P | H | E | R | D | | | |
| R | | | | | | I | | | | | | | |
| | | | | | | A | | | | | | | |
| | | | | | | N | | | | | | | |

21B)

22A) Wish upon a star

22B) Lion King

22C) Running late

22D) Slow motion

22E) Last chance

22F) Give a dog a bone

22G) Under the weather

22H) Bigfoot

## 23A)

| | | | | | | | | | | | | |
|---|---|---|---|---|---|---|---|---|---|---|---|---|
| 1: R | 2: E | 3: A | 4: D | 5: J | 6: F | 7: K | 8: O | 9: N | 10: T | 11: H | 12: Y | 13: I |
| 14: C | 15: P | 16: L | 17: U | 18: X | 19: Q | 20: S | 21: W | 22: V | 23: M | 24: Z | 25: B | 26: G |

## 23B)

| | | | | | | | | | | | | |
|---|---|---|---|---|---|---|---|---|---|---|---|---|
| 1: Q | 2: W | 3: Z | 4: I | 5: O | 6: P | 7: F | 8: D | 9: R | 10: T | 11: A | 12: N | 13: B |
| 14: V | 15: M | 16:C | 17:K | 18: Y | 19: E | 20: G | 21: J | 22: S | 23: U | 24: H | 25: L | 26: X |

24A)

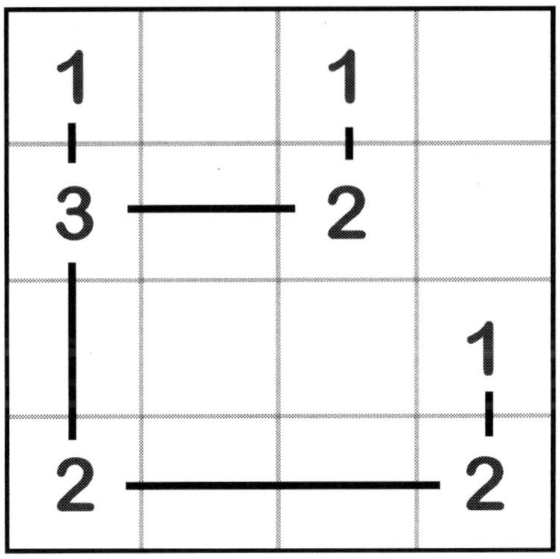

24B)

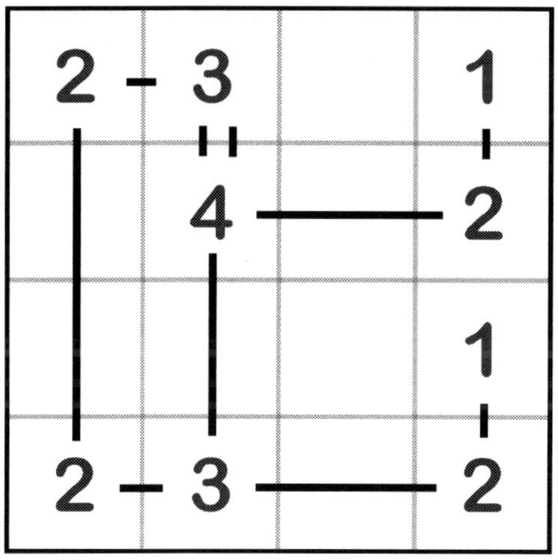

24C)

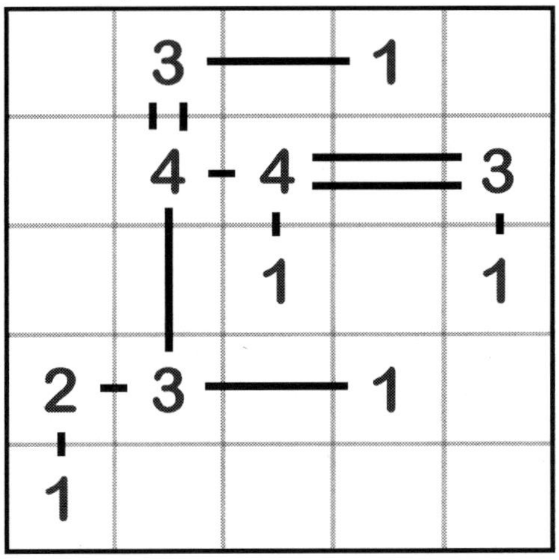

24D)

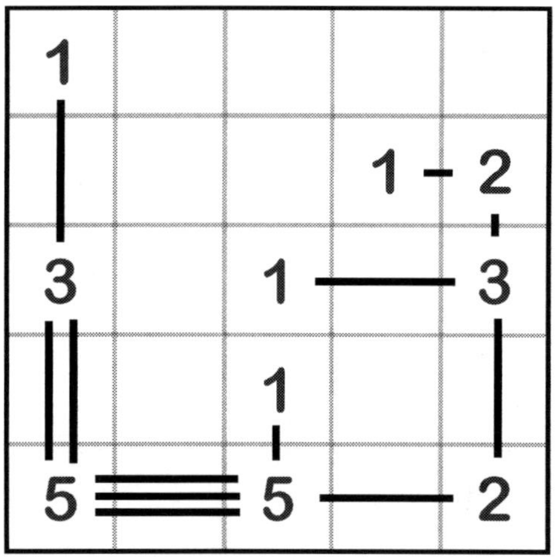

24E)

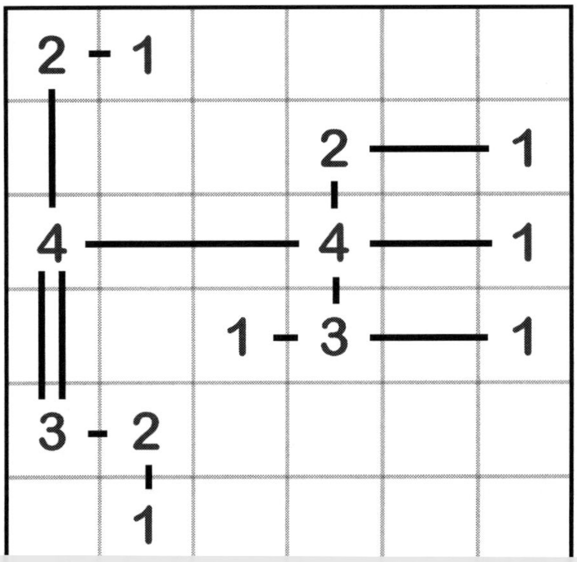

24F)

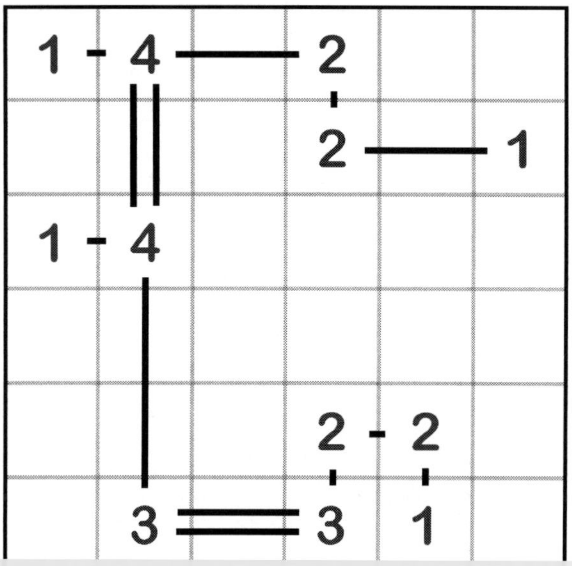

25A)

Young Animals: KID, PUPPY, CUB, KITTEN

Birds: OSTRICH, OWL, PELICAN, EAGLE

Metals: LEAD, TIN, COPPER, IRON

Capitals: BEJING, BANGKOK, PARIS, ATHENS

25B)

Mountains: EVEREST, K2, FUJI, BLANC

Rivers: THAMES, AMAZON, NILE, MISSISSIPPI

Trees: REDWOOD, PINE, WILLOW, OAK

Insect: LOCUST, BUTTERFLY, WASP, MOSQUITO

25C)

Ancient civilisations: AZTEC, ROMAN, GREEK, EGYPTIAN

Numbers backward: ENO, OWT, EERHT, ROUF

Words meaning ‘Big’: LARGE, GIANT, HUGE, MASSIVE

Rhyming: TEA, SEA, BEE, PEA

26A)

| | | | |
|---|---|---|---|
| (12) 4 | 3 | (3) 1 | 2 |
| (2) 2 | 4 | 3 | (3) 1 |
| 1 | (8) 2 | 4 | 3 |
| (3) 3 | 1 | (8) 2 | 4 |

26B)

| | | | |
|---|---|---|---|
| (4) 1 | (12) 3 | 4 | (6) 2 |
| 4 | 2 | (2) 1 | 3 |
| (12) 3 | 4 | 2 | (4) 1 |
| (2) 2 | 1 | 3 | 4 |

26C)

| | | | |
|---|---|---|---|
| 2 | (4) 1 | 4 | (3) 3 |
| (8) 4 | 2 | (6) 3 | 1 |
| (3) 1 | (12) 3 | 2 | (8) 4 |
| 3 | 4 | 1 | 2 |

26D)

| | | | |
|---|---|---|---|
| (12) 3 | 4 | (8) 2 | (2) 1 |
| 1 | (3) 3 | 4 | 2 |
| (8) 2 | 1 | 3 | (12) 4 |
| 4 | (2) 2 | 1 | 3 |

26E)

| | | | | |
|---|---|---|---|---|
| (20) 5 | 4 | (4) 1 | (6) 3 | 2 |
| (3) 1 | 5 | 4 | 2 | (12) 3 |
| 3 | (10) 2 | 5 | (4) 1 | 4 |
| (2) 2 | 1 | 3 | 4 | (5) 5 |
| (12) 4 | 3 | (10) 2 | 5 | 1 |

26F)

| | | | | |
|---|---|---|---|---|
| (3) 1 | (12) 4 | 3 | (10) 2 | (20) 5 |
| 3 | (2) 1 | 2 | 5 | 4 |
| (20) 4 | 5 | (4) 1 | (6) 3 | 2 |
| 5 | (6) 2 | 4 | (3) 1 | 3 |
| 2 | 3 | (20) 5 | 4 | 1 |

27A)

| | | | | | | | | | | | | | | |
|---|---|---|---|---|---|---|---|---|---|---|---|---|---|---|
| G | R | I | U | A | Y | A | S | I | H | O | N | L | A | W |
| S | A | K | N | L | U | O | C | P | N | F | I | R | I | A |
| A | Q | N | A | D | Y | S | O | I | Y | S | A | S | B | P |
| K | C | T | A | K | I | D | T | D | R | E | P | U | I | O |
| G | I | G | P | D | N | A | L | R | S | E | S | F | M | G |
| R | F | X | U | A | A | Q | A | X | A | E | M | L | A | M |
| R | U | M | L | F | B | X | N | Z | V | L | L | A | N | E |
| P | V | G | I | R | O | K | D | P | J | O | I | A | O | X |
| Z | N | J | A | Y | Y | N | A | M | R | E | G | A | W | I |
| E | I | Z | B | L | K | K | A | I | B | M | A | Z | C | C |
| T | I | W | Z | I | I | K | E | N | Y | A | M | E | H | O |
| L | T | E | W | S | M | R | B | I | C | C | F | Y | I | G |
| S | W | I | T | Z | E | R | L | A | N | D | S | N | N | X |
| F | R | A | N | C | E | D | B | J | S | P | E | U | A | H |

27B)

| | | | | | | | | | | | | | | |
|---|---|---|---|---|---|---|---|---|---|---|---|---|---|---|
| C | Q | O | M | M | K | J | L | K | A | Q | R | W | G | I |
| O | T | I | U | Q | L | F | A | R | A | V | W | N | W | B |
| S | G | N | R | H | N | O | C | K | J | B | I | J | F | N |
| W | Z | F | Z | A | X | M | H | O | A | J | U | I | B | C |
| D | I | R | D | A | M | X | M | K | I | R | R | L | N | D |
| H | C | R | U | B | N | I | D | E | C | J | T | F | B | J |
| G | A | R | D | I | F | F | B | K | I | O | K | A | E | W |
| G | A | I | R | O | B | C | U | C | K | W | T | D | R | U |
| O | C | E | F | E | F | W | K | P | N | A | T | S | L | O |
| A | X | R | R | O | L | M | A | D | I | N | V | A | I | R |
| I | W | G | W | O | S | I | B | K | S | N | G | K | N | P |
| D | A | A | N | D | O | N | F | D | L | E | K | L | A | E |
| Z | Y | D | T | V | T | S | J | N | E | I | L | R | M | C |
| B | O | S | N | T | K | K | U | S | H | V | I | O | C | B |
| N | S | D | H | I | O | P | X | B | W | S | R | M | S | F |

28A) Carpet

28B) An Umbrella

28C) A Clock

28D) A Stick

28E) A Road

28F) A Fence

28G) Tomorrow

28H) Just One

28I) A Glove

28J) Light

28K) A Sponge

28L) A Balloon

28M) They live in the Southern Hemisphere

28N) A Pair of Shoes

28O) Cutlery

28P) A Keyhole

28Q) Freeze the water

28R) Your Breath

29A)

| | | | |
|---|---|---|---|
| 11 | 10 | 7 | 6 |
| 12 | 9 | 8 | 5 |
| 13 | 16 | 3 | 4 |
| 14 | 15 | 2 | 1 |

29B)

| | | | |
|---|---|---|---|
| 9 | 10 | 11 | 12 |
| 8 | 7 | 16 | 13 |
| 5 | 6 | 15 | 14 |
| 4 | 3 | 2 | 1 |

29C)

| | | | |
|---|---|---|---|
| 2 | 3 | 4 | 5 |
| 1 | 10 | 9 | 6 |
| 12 | 11 | 8 | 7 |
| 13 | 14 | 15 | 16 |

29D)

| | | | |
|---|---|---|---|
| 1 | 3 | 6 | 7 |
| 2 | 4 | 5 | 8 |
| 14 | 15 | 16 | 9 |
| 13 | 12 | 11 | 10 |

29E)

| | | | | |
|---|---|---|---|---|
| 23 | 24 | 2 | 1 | 5 |
| 22 | 25 | 3 | 4 | 6 |
| 21 | 20 | 12 | 11 | 7 |
| 18 | 19 | 13 | 10 | 8 |
| 17 | 16 | 15 | 14 | 9 |

29F)

| | | | | |
|---|---|---|---|---|
| 1 | 16 | 18 | 19 | 21 |
| 2 | 15 | 17 | 20 | 22 |
| 3 | 14 | 13 | 12 | 23 |
| 4 | 7 | 8 | 11 | 24 |
| 5 | 6 | 9 | 10 | 25 |

## 30A)

| | | | | | | | | |
|---|---|---|---|---|---|---|---|---|
| 9 | 3 | 8 | 2 | 5 | 6 | 7 | 1 | 4 |
| 1 | 4 | 7 | 9 | 3 | 8 | 6 | 2 | 5 |
| 6 | 5 | 2 | 1 | 4 | 7 | 9 | 3 | 8 |
| 2 | 6 | 3 | 8 | 9 | 1 | 5 | 4 | 7 |
| 7 | 1 | 9 | 4 | 6 | 5 | 3 | 8 | 2 |
| 5 | 8 | 4 | 7 | 2 | 3 | 1 | 6 | 9 |
| 4 | 9 | 5 | 3 | 1 | 2 | 8 | 7 | 6 |
| 8 | 2 | 1 | 6 | 7 | 9 | 4 | 5 | 3 |
| 3 | 7 | 6 | 5 | 8 | 4 | 2 | 9 | 1 |

## 30B)

| | | | | | | | | |
|---|---|---|---|---|---|---|---|---|
| 3 | 8 | 7 | 9 | 6 | 1 | 5 | 4 | 2 |
| 9 | 4 | 1 | 7 | 5 | 2 | 8 | 3 | 6 |
| 2 | 6 | 5 | 3 | 8 | 4 | 1 | 9 | 7 |
| 4 | 9 | 8 | 2 | 1 | 6 | 7 | 5 | 3 |
| 7 | 5 | 3 | 4 | 9 | 8 | 6 | 2 | 1 |
| 6 | 1 | 2 | 5 | 3 | 7 | 4 | 8 | 9 |
| 1 | 7 | 9 | 8 | 2 | 5 | 3 | 6 | 4 |
| 5 | 3 | 4 | 6 | 7 | 9 | 2 | 1 | 8 |
| 8 | 2 | 6 | 1 | 4 | 3 | 9 | 7 | 5 |

## 30C)

| | | | | | | | | |
|---|---|---|---|---|---|---|---|---|
| 5 | 9 | 7 | 4 | 3 | 2 | 1 | 8 | 6 |
| 6 | 2 | 1 | 5 | 7 | 8 | 3 | 4 | 9 |
| 3 | 4 | 8 | 9 | 1 | 6 | 7 | 5 | 2 |
| 8 | 3 | 6 | 7 | 5 | 1 | 9 | 2 | 4 |
| 2 | 1 | 5 | 8 | 4 | 9 | 6 | 3 | 7 |
| 4 | 7 | 9 | 2 | 6 | 3 | 8 | 1 | 5 |
| 9 | 5 | 4 | 1 | 8 | 7 | 2 | 6 | 3 |
| 7 | 8 | 3 | 6 | 2 | 4 | 5 | 9 | 1 |
| 1 | 6 | 2 | 3 | 9 | 5 | 4 | 7 | 8 |

## 30D)

| | | | | | | | | |
|---|---|---|---|---|---|---|---|---|
| 2 | 5 | 7 | 9 | 4 | 6 | 8 | 3 | 1 |
| 9 | 4 | 3 | 2 | 8 | 1 | 6 | 5 | 7 |
| 1 | 8 | 6 | 5 | 3 | 7 | 2 | 9 | 4 |
| 5 | 7 | 9 | 1 | 2 | 8 | 3 | 4 | 6 |
| 6 | 1 | 2 | 3 | 5 | 4 | 9 | 7 | 8 |
| 8 | 3 | 4 | 6 | 7 | 9 | 1 | 2 | 5 |
| 4 | 9 | 5 | 8 | 1 | 3 | 7 | 6 | 2 |
| 3 | 2 | 1 | 7 | 6 | 5 | 4 | 8 | 9 |
| 7 | 6 | 8 | 4 | 9 | 2 | 5 | 1 | 3 |

## 30E)

| | | | | | | | | |
|---|---|---|---|---|---|---|---|---|
| 5 | 9 | 7 | 8 | 3 | 1 | 6 | 4 | 2 |
| 2 | 4 | 8 | 9 | 5 | 6 | 1 | 7 | 3 |
| 6 | 1 | 3 | 2 | 7 | 4 | 5 | 9 | 8 |
| 1 | 6 | 5 | 7 | 4 | 3 | 8 | 2 | 9 |
| 8 | 2 | 4 | 1 | 6 | 9 | 3 | 5 | 7 |
| 7 | 3 | 9 | 5 | 2 | 8 | 4 | 1 | 6 |
| 3 | 8 | 1 | 4 | 9 | 7 | 2 | 6 | 5 |
| 4 | 7 | 2 | 6 | 8 | 5 | 9 | 3 | 1 |
| 9 | 5 | 6 | 3 | 1 | 2 | 7 | 8 | 4 |

## 30F)

| | | | | | | | | |
|---|---|---|---|---|---|---|---|---|
| 7 | 4 | 5 | 6 | 2 | 1 | 3 | 8 | 9 |
| 8 | 9 | 2 | 7 | 5 | 3 | 1 | 6 | 4 |
| 1 | 6 | 3 | 4 | 9 | 8 | 5 | 7 | 2 |
| 6 | 5 | 8 | 1 | 7 | 9 | 2 | 4 | 3 |
| 4 | 3 | 1 | 8 | 6 | 2 | 7 | 9 | 5 |
| 2 | 7 | 9 | 3 | 4 | 5 | 6 | 1 | 8 |
| 9 | 1 | 4 | 5 | 3 | 7 | 8 | 2 | 6 |
| 5 | 8 | 6 | 2 | 1 | 4 | 9 | 3 | 7 |
| 3 | 2 | 7 | 9 | 8 | 6 | 4 | 5 | 1 |

31A)

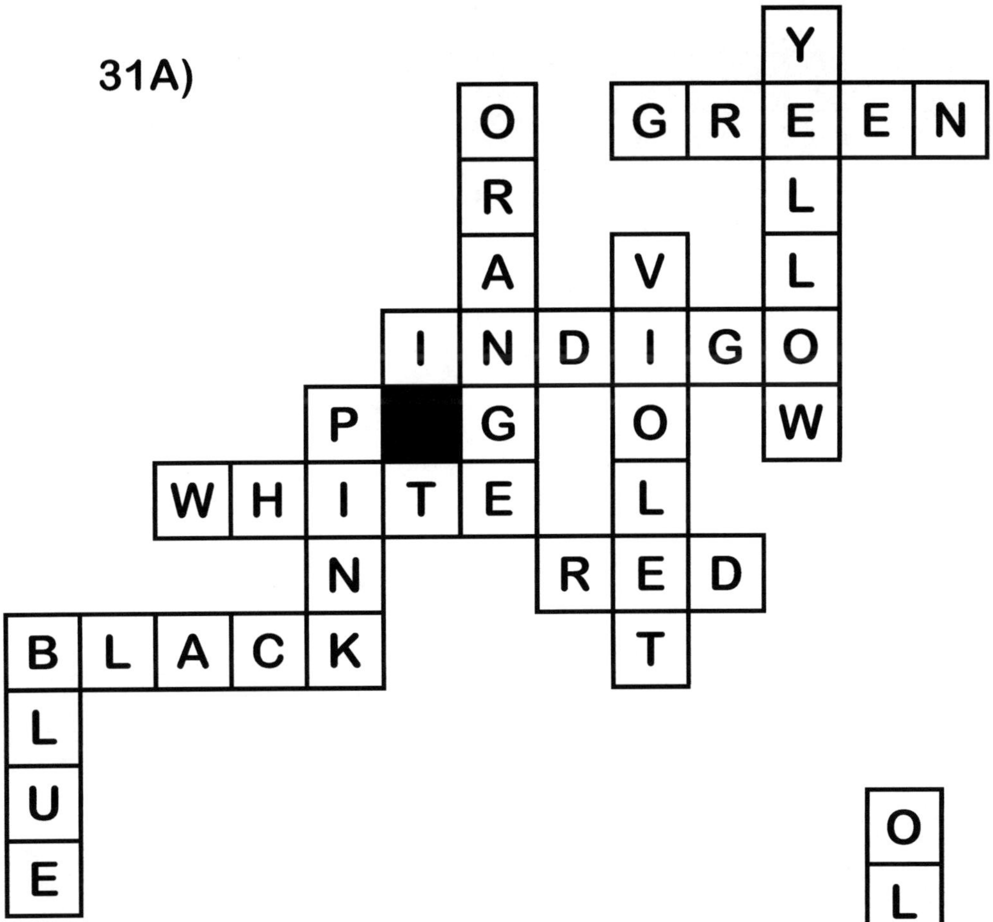
GREEN
YELLOW
ORANGE
VIOLET
INDIGO
PINK
WHITE
RED
BLACK
BLUE

31B)

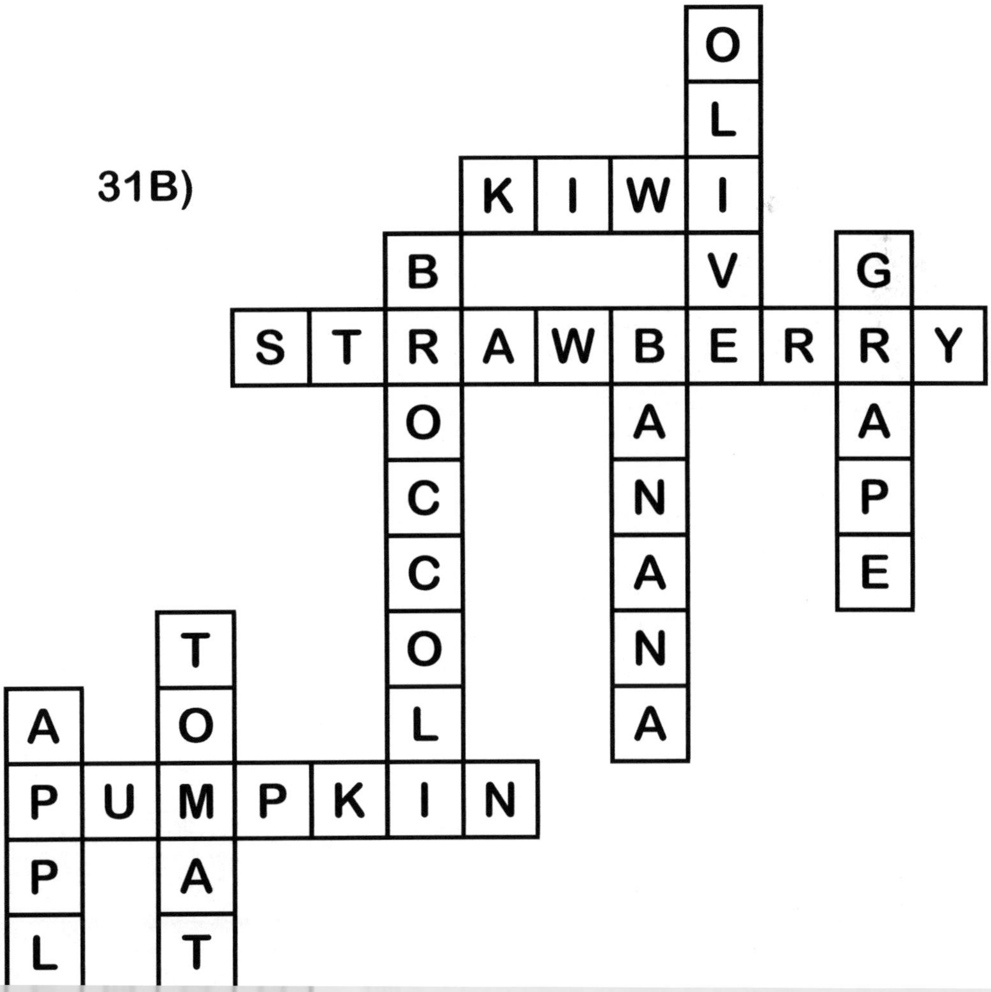
OLIVE
KIWI
BROCCOLI
STRAWBERRY
GRAPE
BANANA
TOMAT
APPL
PUMPKIN

## 32A)

| | | | | | | | | |
|---|---|---|---|---|---|---|---|---|
| 7 | 4 | 5 | 6 | 9 | 1 | 2 | 3 | 8 |
| 8 | 1 | 6 | 3 | 2 | 5 | 7 | 4 | 9 |
| 3 | 9 | 2 | 7 | 8 | 4 | 5 | 1 | 6 |
| 5 | 2 | 3 | 1 | 6 | 7 | 9 | 8 | 4 |
| 4 | 6 | 9 | 8 | 5 | 3 | 1 | 7 | 2 |
| 1 | 7 | 8 | 2 | 4 | 9 | 6 | 5 | 3 |
| 2 | 5 | 7 | 9 | 3 | 8 | 4 | 6 | 1 |
| 9 | 8 | 4 | 5 | 1 | 6 | 3 | 2 | 7 |
| 6 | 3 | 1 | 4 | 7 | 2 | 8 | 9 | 5 |

## 32B)

| | | | | | | | | |
|---|---|---|---|---|---|---|---|---|
| 8 | 9 | 6 | 2 | 5 | 1 | 4 | 3 | 7 |
| 1 | 7 | 4 | 3 | 6 | 9 | 2 | 5 | 8 |
| 5 | 2 | 3 | 4 | 8 | 7 | 1 | 9 | 6 |
| 9 | 1 | 5 | 8 | 3 | 2 | 7 | 6 | 4 |
| 6 | 8 | 7 | 5 | 9 | 4 | 3 | 1 | 2 |
| 3 | 4 | 2 | 7 | 1 | 6 | 9 | 8 | 5 |
| 4 | 5 | 8 | 9 | 7 | 3 | 6 | 2 | 1 |
| 7 | 6 | 9 | 1 | 2 | 8 | 5 | 4 | 3 |
| 2 | 3 | 1 | 6 | 4 | 5 | 8 | 7 | 9 |

## 32C)

| | | | | | | | | |
|---|---|---|---|---|---|---|---|---|
| 5 | 4 | 8 | 2 | 3 | 1 | 9 | 7 | 6 |
| 7 | 1 | 9 | 5 | 4 | 6 | 3 | 8 | 2 |
| 3 | 2 | 6 | 9 | 8 | 7 | 5 | 1 | 4 |
| 1 | 5 | 3 | 7 | 6 | 2 | 8 | 4 | 9 |
| 8 | 9 | 7 | 3 | 5 | 4 | 6 | 2 | 1 |
| 4 | 6 | 2 | 1 | 9 | 8 | 7 | 3 | 5 |
| 6 | 3 | 1 | 8 | 2 | 5 | 4 | 9 | 7 |
| 9 | 7 | 4 | 6 | 1 | 3 | 2 | 5 | 8 |
| 2 | 8 | 5 | 4 | 7 | 9 | 1 | 6 | 3 |

## 32D)

| | | | | | | | | |
|---|---|---|---|---|---|---|---|---|
| 3 | 5 | 4 | 7 | 8 | 2 | 9 | 6 | 1 |
| 8 | 6 | 1 | 5 | 3 | 9 | 2 | 7 | 4 |
| 7 | 2 | 9 | 1 | 4 | 6 | 3 | 5 | 8 |
| 6 | 3 | 2 | 4 | 5 | 1 | 8 | 9 | 7 |
| 1 | 9 | 7 | 8 | 6 | 3 | 4 | 2 | 5 |
| 5 | 4 | 8 | 9 | 2 | 7 | 1 | 3 | 6 |
| 4 | 1 | 6 | 3 | 9 | 5 | 7 | 8 | 2 |
| 2 | 7 | 3 | 6 | 1 | 8 | 5 | 4 | 9 |
| 9 | 8 | 5 | 2 | 7 | 4 | 6 | 1 | 3 |

## 32E)

| | | | | | | | | |
|---|---|---|---|---|---|---|---|---|
| 8 | 5 | 3 | 7 | 6 | 9 | 2 | 4 | 1 |
| 7 | 4 | 9 | 2 | 8 | 1 | 3 | 6 | 5 |
| 6 | 2 | 1 | 5 | 3 | 4 | 8 | 7 | 9 |
| 9 | 8 | 2 | 6 | 4 | 3 | 5 | 1 | 7 |
| 4 | 6 | 7 | 1 | 5 | 2 | 9 | 3 | 8 |
| 3 | 1 | 5 | 8 | 9 | 7 | 6 | 2 | 4 |
| 2 | 9 | 4 | 3 | 1 | 5 | 7 | 8 | 6 |
| 5 | 7 | 6 | 4 | 2 | 8 | 1 | 9 | 3 |
| 1 | 3 | 8 | 9 | 7 | 6 | 4 | 5 | 2 |

## 32F)

| | | | | | | | | |
|---|---|---|---|---|---|---|---|---|
| 4 | 5 | 1 | 6 | 2 | 7 | 9 | 3 | 8 |
| 6 | 8 | 7 | 9 | 3 | 5 | 2 | 1 | 4 |
| 3 | 9 | 2 | 1 | 4 | 8 | 6 | 5 | 7 |
| 5 | 1 | 6 | 2 | 8 | 9 | 4 | 7 | 3 |
| 8 | 2 | 4 | 5 | 7 | 3 | 1 | 6 | 9 |
| 7 | 3 | 9 | 4 | 1 | 6 | 8 | 2 | 5 |
| 1 | 6 | 8 | 7 | 5 | 4 | 3 | 9 | 2 |
| 9 | 4 | 5 | 3 | 6 | 2 | 7 | 8 | 1 |
| 2 | 7 | 3 | 8 | 9 | 1 | 5 | 4 | 6 |

33A): Asia

33B): A Herd

33C): Cheetah

33D): Blue Whale

33E): Asia

33F): China

33G): Sahara

33H): Five Oceans

33I): Vatican City

33J): India

33K): The Great Barrier Reef

33L): Jupiter

33M): Water

33N): Cats

33O): Beavers

33P): Mars

34A)

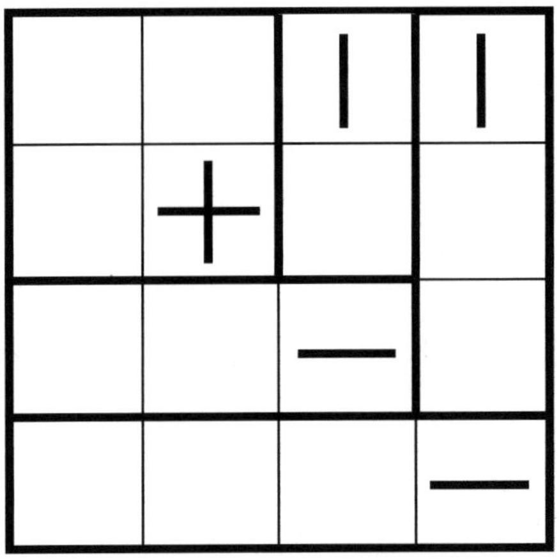

34B)

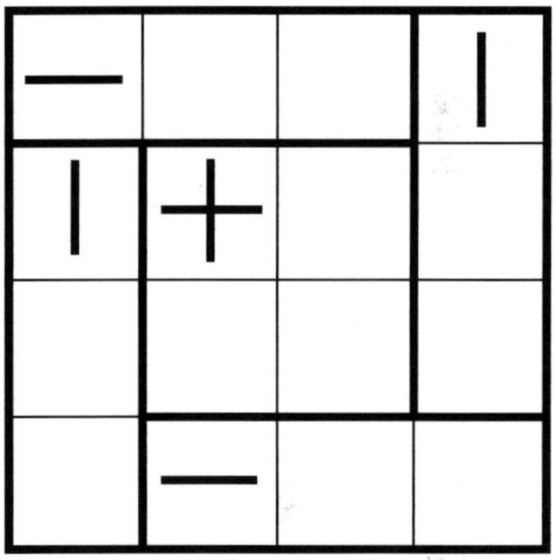

34C)

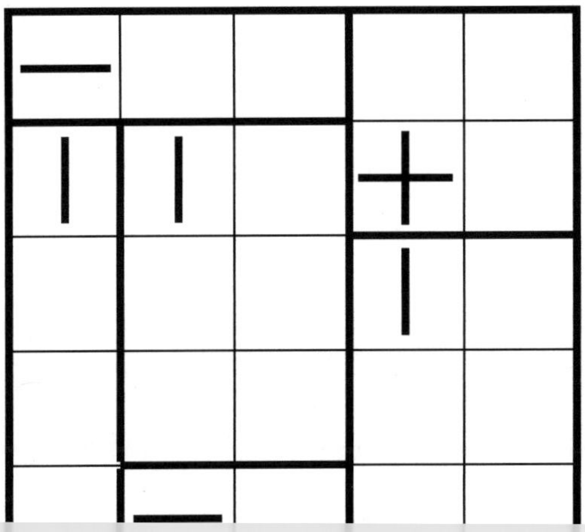

34D)

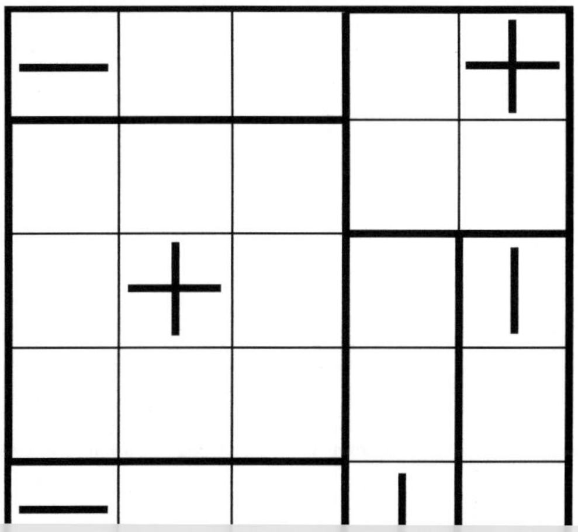

34E)

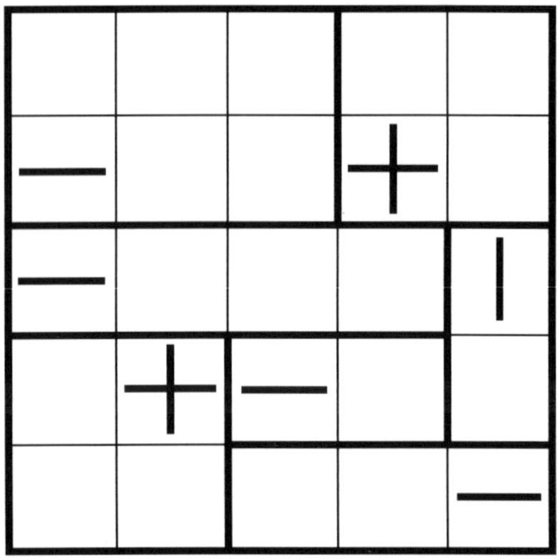

34F)

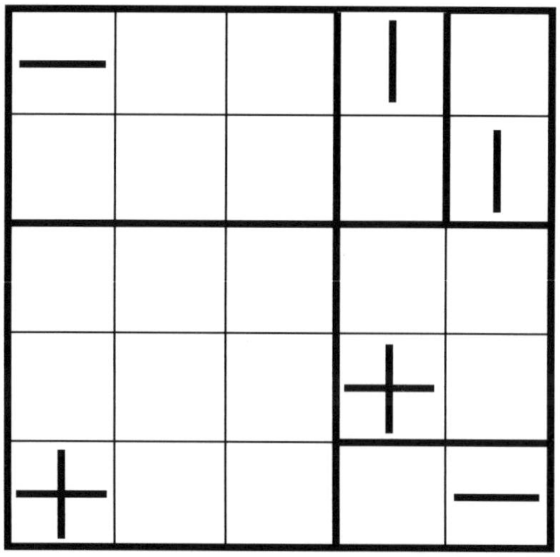

35A)

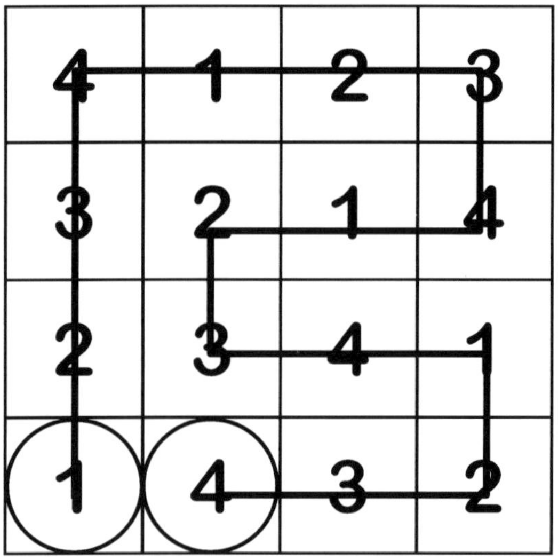

35B)

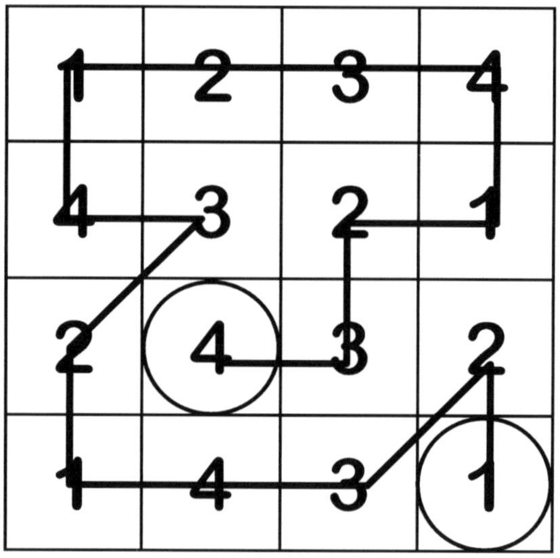

35C)

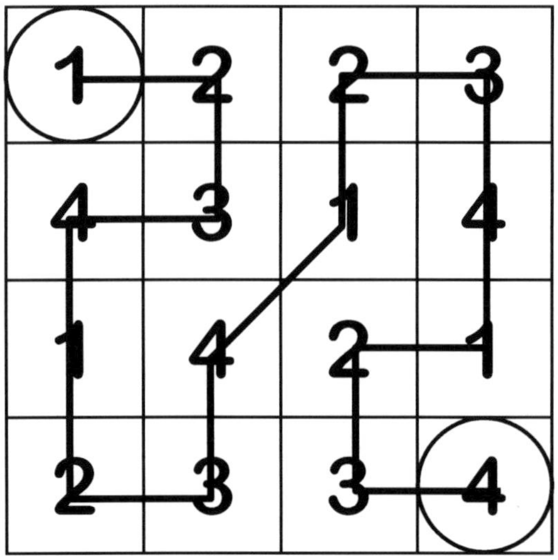

35D)

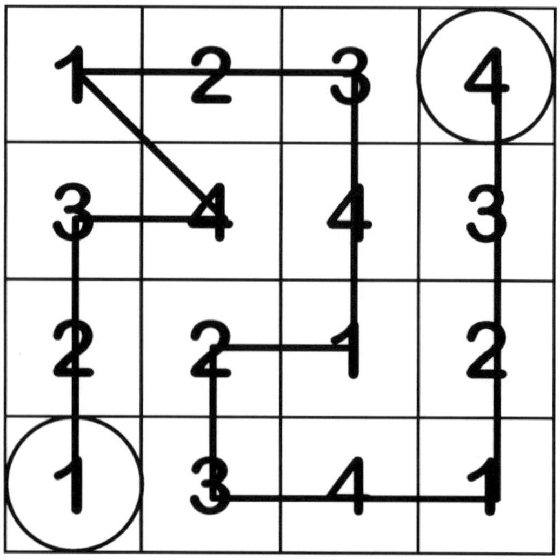

35E)

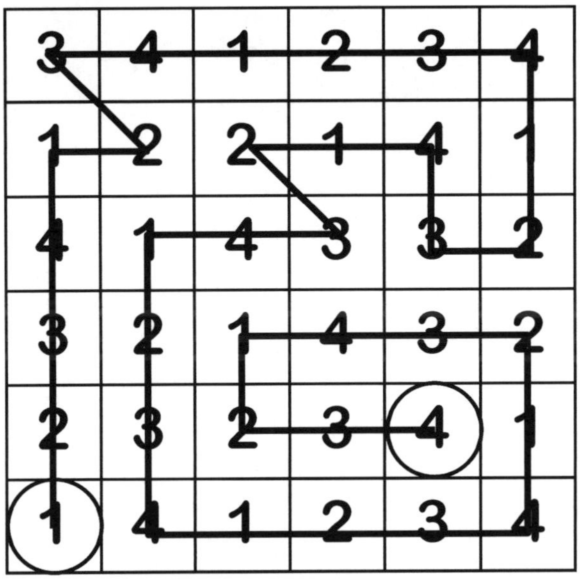

35F)

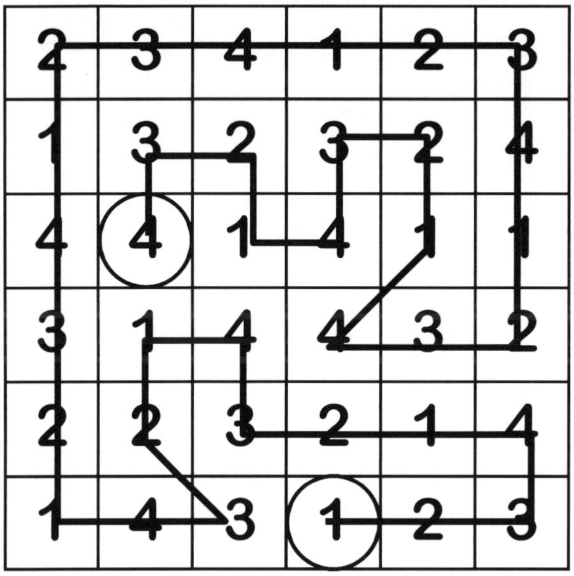

36A) The Olympics started in GREECE

The capital of France is PARIS

We need to breathe in OXYGEN to survive

MARS is also known as the Red Planet

36B) SWEDEN is the only Scandinavian country beginning with S

HORSE chestnuts are also called conkers

WWW stands for WORLD Wide Web

GARGOYLES are the stone statues found on churches

37A) Hamburg has over 2,300 bridges - the most in the world

37B) The Jigsaw had 551,232 pieces, and was a picture of a lotus

37C) 46,001 press ups in a day is more than one every two seconds

37D) Jeanne Louise Calment lived for 122 years, 164 days. She was one year old when the telephone was invented, and lived to see DVDs

37E) A single cubic inch contains one million grains of sand

37F) Americans drink 400 million cups of coffee every single day

37G) Lego produce 700 million tyres each year, more than double

**38A)**

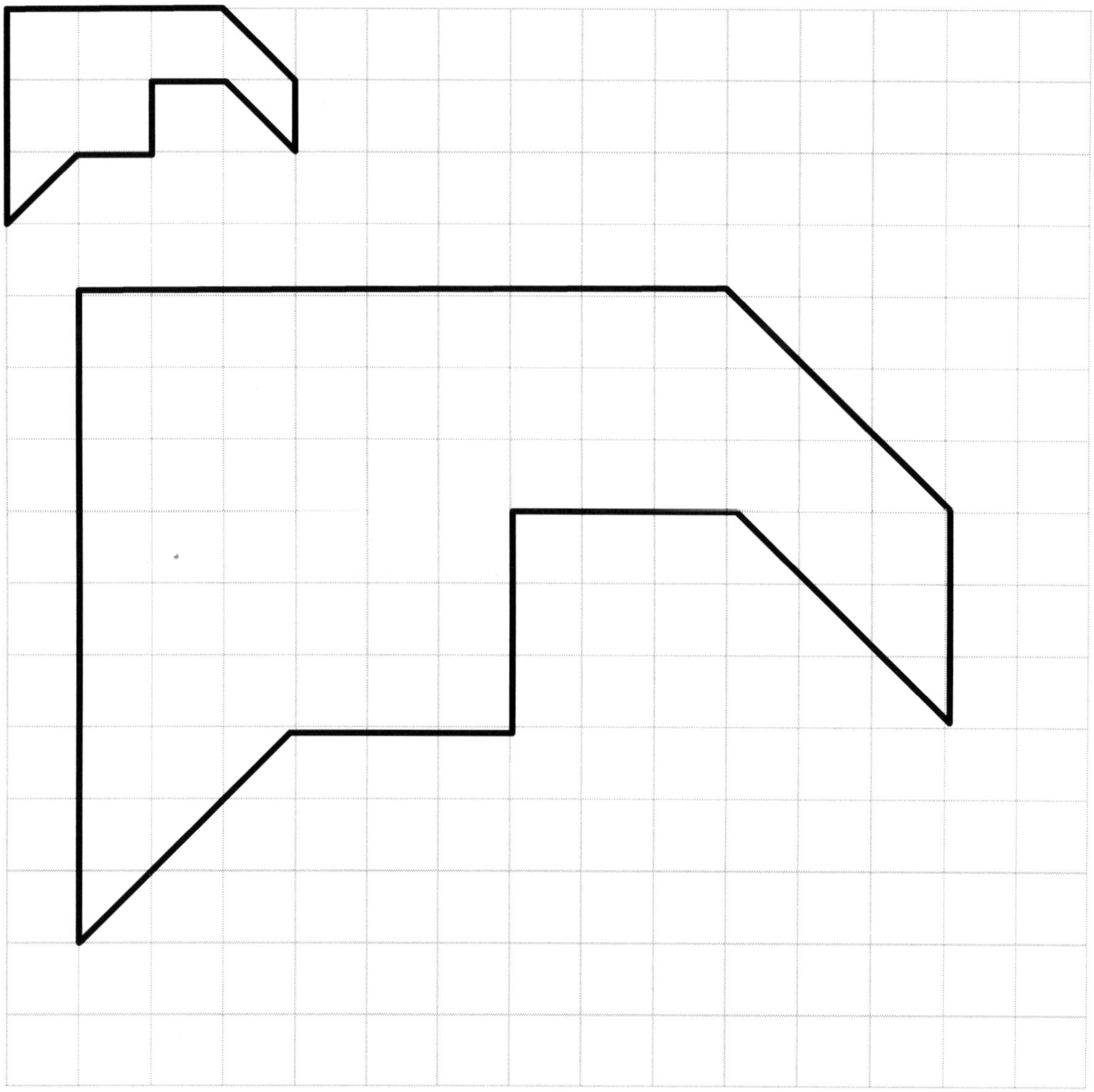

**38B)**

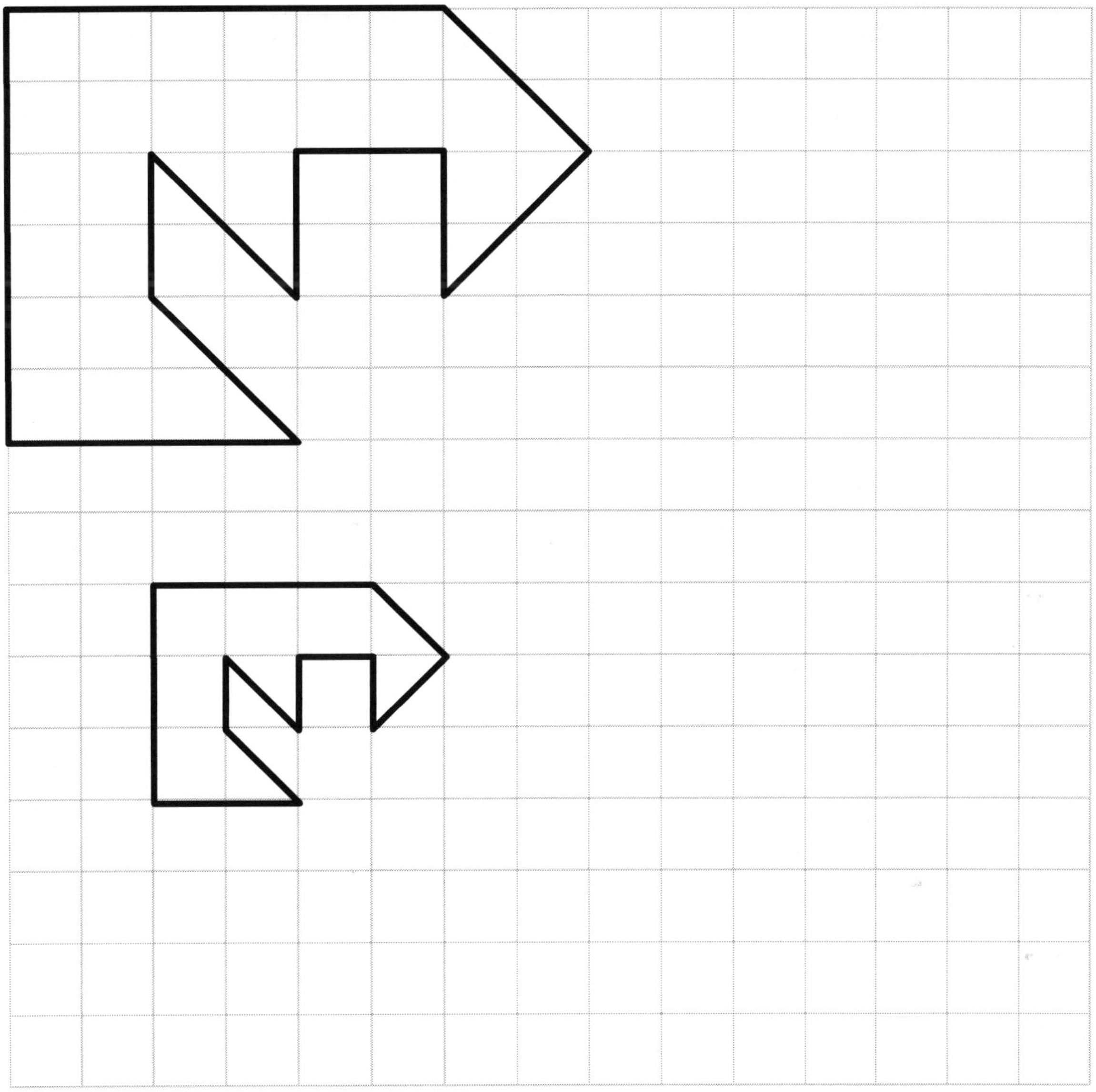

39A) TURKEY

39B) PRESENTS

39C) HOLIDAY

39D) TREE

39E) SANTA

39F) PUDDING

39G) BAUBLE

39H) ANGEL

39I) RUDOLPH

39K) CRACKER

39L) REINDEER

39M) LION

39N) TIGER

39O) GIRAFFE

39P) MONKEY

39Q) ELEPHANT

39R) RHINO

39S) MEERKAT

39U) BEAR

39V) WOLF

39W) JAMES

39Y) ALEX

39Z) ADAM

39AA) DAVID

39AB) GEORGE

39AC) CHARLOTTE

39AD) ALICE

40A)

| | | | |
|---|---|---|---|
| 2 | 3 | | 1 |
| 2 | 1 | 1 | 3 |
| | 2 | 2 | 3 |
| 2 | 3 | 1 | |

40B)

| | | | |
|---|---|---|---|
| 2 | | 2 | 3 |
| 1 | 3 | 1 | 3 |
| | 1 | 2 | 3 |
| 1 | 1 | 3 | |

40C)

| | | | |
|---|---|---|---|
| | 1 | 1 | 2 |
| 3 | | 3 | 1 |
| 2 | 2 | 3 | 3 |
| 3 | 2 | | 2 |

40D)

| | | | |
|---|---|---|---|
| 2 | 1 | 3 | |
| 3 | | 3 | 2 |
| | 1 | 1 | 1 |
| 2 | 1 | | 3 |

40E)

| | | | | |
|---|---|---|---|---|
| 2 | 2 | | 1 | 3 |
| | 2 | 1 | 3 | 3 |
| 3 | | 3 | 1 | |
| 1 | 1 | 1 | | 1 |
| 2 | 3 | 1 | 3 | 1 |

40F)

| | | | | |
|---|---|---|---|---|
| 1 | 1 | | 2 | 3 |
| | 2 | 3 | 1 | 2 |
| 3 | 1 | 3 | 3 | |
| 3 | | 3 | 2 | 1 |
| 3 | 2 | 2 | | 1 |

Manufactured by Amazon.ca
Bolton, ON

34119525R00063